It's My Prerogative!

McDougal & Associates
Servants of Christ and stewards of the mysteries of God

Endorsements

"First I would like to say how proud I am of you, my sister and best friend. This is just the beginning of the way you will bless the lives of many women, especially pastors' wives. This book will echo the opinion of many who have much to say but, for one reason or another, are not able to say it. I especially love your Chapter 24. Historically far too many pastors have been drawn into sin because of their work in counseling troubled women. It's time that we become wiser in this regard. Maybe, as you suggest, we should refer many of these women to licensed professionals who can help them with their sexual, emotional and marital problems. After all, our pastors are not supermen."

First Lady Tawana Rose
The Life Church
Houston, Texas

"Congratulations, Lady Gayle Woodard, on your divine endeavor with this book. I'm a pastor's kid or PK as we're so often called, and I can identify with the sentiments you've expressed about their plight. I'm so grateful that someone is willing to take a stand for PKs, and I recommend this book to PKs everywhere! By reading it, you will be inspired, exhilarated and refreshed, and your life will be changed."

Cakeema Easterling
Queens, New York

"Gayle Woodard is a gift to the Body of Christ. Her genuine love for women and pastors' wives in particular was poured into her heart from God Himself. The lives of many women from around the country are enriched by her encouraging ministry."

First Lady Sheretta M. West
The Church Without Walls
Houston, Texas

"To my sweet, anointed and dear sister: Although some see the glitz and the glamour and may even aspire to the role of the first lady, you have the personal experience, along with other first ladies, to know the challenges and the keen anointing required for this awesome task. Thank you for letting your readers take a small glimpse into the many faces and hats we wear and the burdens we sometimes encounter as a first lady. Serving as a first lady is an awesome task that one must be called to fulfill, but it is also a great joy to become the intercessor for an anointed man of God."

First Lady Alfredia Lee
Greater Vision Church
Houston, Texas

"I thank God so much for this book concerning first ladies. I know this is going to be a blessing, not only to all first ladies, but also to the entire Body of Christ. It is imperative for all first ladies to understand their role in Christ and to follow the model, as set forth in the Bible. This book will demonstrate just how significant the office of a first lady is."

First Lady Debbie E. Hawkins
Voices of Faith Ministries
Stone Mountain, Georgia

"As a radio announcer, I've met many first ladies and women in ministry, but I can say that I've come across a true woman of God in First Lady Gayle Woodard. She has a genuine concern for all women, and her awesome vision of helping women is reflected in the way she is always willing to give of herself. It is with great respect and honor that I endorse this book that I know will be a blessing to all who read it."

Letitia "Tish" Jackson
Host of Wings of Faith Morning Show on KWWJ
Houston, TX, Baytown, TX, Galveston, TX and
KZZB, Beaumont, TX and Port Arthur, TX

"First Lady Gayle is one of the strong, powerful and spiritual minds of this twenty-first century, and she embodies in herself the great presence of a leader. I am so happy to know that now the rest of the world will get an opportunity to experience pieces of her greatness through this book. Congratulations!"

Kim Burrell
Houston, Texas

It's My Prerogative!

Standing by Your Man in Ministry

by

Lady Gayle Woodard

Unless otherwise noted, all references are from *The New International Version of the Bible,* copyright © 1973, 1978, 1984 by International Bible Society, Colorado Springs, Colorado. References marked NKJ are from *The New King James Version of the Bible,* copyright © 1979, 1980, 1982, by Thomas Nelson, Inc., Nashville, Tennessee. References marked NLT are from *The New Living Translation of the Bible,* copyright © 1996 by Tyndale House Publishers, Inc., Wheaton, Illinois. References marked KJV are from the *King James Version of the Bible.* The definitions on the Definitions page are from dictionary.com. The definitions within the acrostic in Chapter 23 are from *Webster's Dictionary of the English Language.* The definition in Chapter 20 is from reference.com.

Published by:

McDougal & Associates
P.O. Box 194
Greenwell Springs, LA 70739-0194
www.thepublishedword.com

McDougal & Associates is dedicated to the spreading of the Gospel of Jesus Christ to as many people as possible in the shortest time possible.

ISBN 13: 978-1-934769-07-2
ISBN 10: 1-934769-07-X
Printed in the United States of America
For Worldwide Distribution

Dedication

I would like to dedicate this book to my soulmate, best friend and husband, *Pastor Leroy Woodard, Jr.* You are the best husband in the world and a great dad to our sons. Thank you for believing in me, always speaking into my life and encouraging me. You are my personal motivation, as well as my pastor and an awesome preacher/teacher. I can truly say that you are a man who not only preaches and teaches the Word of God, but also lives it, and you make it easy for me to stand beside you in ministry. I'm so honored to do it and so appreciative of your love, support and prayers. You have my everlasting love.

Your Only Lady,
Gayle

To my Lord and Savior, *Jesus Christ*, who is the Author and Finisher of my life. You gave me the wisdom and knowledge I needed to write this book. I praise You and magnify Your name. Thank You, Lord.

I would like to dedicate Chapter 18, Making Time for Healing, to my best friend and sister in the flesh, *Lady Tawana Rose*. May this chapter encourage and empower you. You know that the God we serve is an incredible God. He has already worked a miracle in your mind, your body and your soul. So receive your total healing.

You have poured out into the lives of so many people with your love, your sense of humor and your giving spirit. God has not brought you this far to leave you now. He is honored by your faith, your intercessory prayer, your giving spirit and your genuine love for others.

I have made a personal covenant with God for your healing. Words can't express the unconditional love that I have for you, my sister. You go, Girl! Your healing is an accomplished fact! It's done, in Jesus' name!

Acknowledgments

To my sisters in Christ and Koinonia Book Club members Delinda Mackey, Ariana Rogers, Barbara Wilson (Minister Deric Wilson), Sheila Austin (Brother Anthony Austin) and Phyllis Simpson (Minister Ron Simpson): I wrote this book on a divine assignment from God. I knew that it was the appropriate season for the information it contains, but as I began to write, there were just not enough hours in the day. Then God revealed to me the names of those who were to assist me in completing this assignment. Thank you from the bottom of my heart for the time and passion you all have put into this project to make it a success. May God continue to bless you. Remember, only what you do for Christ will last.

To my Armor Bearer Ministry: Thanks for all your prayers and support—Suzette Lartique, Betsy McGuire, Mary Alice Gordon, Dawn Thomas, Cynthia Paige and Reba Powell.

To Oprah Winfrey: Thank you. Your show has been an inspiration to my life.

To Marcus and Joni Lamb at Daystar Television: You have been a blessing to people all over the world. Please continue to spread God's Word through your television ministry. It has been an honor for Pastor Woodard and me to host one of your shows.

To the memory of my father-in-law, the Late Bishop L.J. Woodard, and to my mother-in-law, Future Woodard: Thanks for being a wonderful mother-in-law and for the many times you picked the grandkids up from school and spoiled them.

To Bishop Osha Randle, Sr. and Lady Doris Randle, my God-blessed mother: Thank you for your love and for teaching me how to be that Proverbs 31:10 woman.

To Leroy Woodard, Jr. and Demond Woodard: You are the greatest sons a mother could ever ask for. Thank you for your love and support. Continue to stay focused and prayerful. I love you with a mother's unconditional love.

My gratitude goes out to Pastor Leroy Woodard, II, the CRM City Fellowship church family and staff, Bishop Gene Moore, Sr., Bishop T.D Jakes and Lady Serita Jakes, Pastor Ralph West and Lady Sherita West, Bishop Gary Hawkins, Sr. and Lady Debbie Hawkins, Pastor Terrence Cooper and Lady Valerie Cooper, Pastor Robert Allen and Lady Shaun Allen, Pastor Patrick Suphen, Bishop Richard Rose and Lady Tawana Rose, Pastor LeKeith Lee and Lady Alfredia Lee, Leticia Jackson (The Queen of Gospel 1360), Pastor Anthony Rogers and Lady Debra Rogers, Kelly Price and husband Jeffrey, Kim Burrell, Pastor Marvin Sapp and Lady Sapp, Bishop I. V. Hilliard and Lady Bridgett Hilliard, Pastor Joel Osteen and Lady Victoria Osteen, Pastor Janet Floyd, my father, Reverend

John Rogers and Gwen Rogers, my brother- and sister-in-law Warren and Gladys Hawkins, My Sorors in the Koinonia Sorority, Karen Jackson and the Sisters Network, my brother Minister John Rogers and Ariana Rogers, my brother Mathis Rogers, Pastor Edwards and Lady Edwards, Pastor Thurman Graves and Lady Graves, Jerry and Mary Brumfield and family, Louis and Juanita Mitchell, Mr. and Mrs. Arthur L. and Debbie Andrews, Minister Ron and Phyllis Simpson, Mr. and Mrs. Don and Anna Hill, the late Minister James Williams and wife, Martha Williams, Pastor Remus Wright and Lady Mia Wright, Pastor Manson Johnson and Lady Johnson, Pastor Tai Paschall and Lady Paschall, Mr. Harris and Mrs. Ruby Harris, Craig Amos (CBA Media/Book Cover Designer), Patryce Coleman (Photographer), Darryl Martin (President of Gospel 1360), Reba Powell, Helen Cockerell, Attorney Jalene Mack, Lea Rutherford-Williams, Yolanda Adams and Leonard and Dorothy Jones.

To TBN: Thank you. Your television ministry has been a blessing all over the world. The movie *Easter* was phenomenal. Continue to spread the Gospel of Jesus Christ.

To my Goddaughters, Christian Spears, Raivyn Hearn and Elizabeth Adams: I love you. Thanks for being wonderful goddaughters to me.

To my nieces and nephews: I am grateful to you. You're the best. Nieces: Narissa Rogers, Demeria Rogers, Arielle Rogers, Kennedy Lee, Alecina Rogers and Karington Lee. Nephews: Aaron Rogers, Billy Howard, Jr., Christopher Dargin, Broderick Bonton, John Rogers, Jr., Stephen

Dargin and Phillip Dargin. Continue to be great children in school, stay focused, obey your parents, always pray and remember the promise of Philippians 4:13: *"I can do all things through Christ who strengthens me"* (NKJ).

A special thanks goes to my grandparents. Thanks to Lucile Reece (Momma Lucile) for your love and support and your home-style old-fashioned cooking and Victoria Jackson (Grandmother) for all of your love and home-cooked greens and corn bread. In loving memory of Nita Cooks (Momma Nita). I will never forget your words of wisdom, your delicious fruits and your homemade moist lemon cakes.

With this book, I would also like to honor the following first ladies: First Lady of our nation, Laura Bush, First Lady of our great state of Texas, Anita Perry, former First Lady Hillary Clinton and the first ladies of the recent campaign: Cindy McCain and First Lady Michelle Obama, wife of President-Elect Barack Obama.

Contents

Definitions

Prerogative: "an exclusive right, privilege, etc., exercised by virtue of rank, office, or the like: *the prerogatives of a senator.* A right, privilege, etc., limited to a specific person or to persons of a particular category: *It was the teacher's prerogative to stop the discussion.*"

First Lady: "The wife of the president of the United States or of the governor of a state. The wife of the head of any country: *the First Lady of Brazil.* The foremost woman in any art, profession, or the like: *First Lady of the American theater.* The wife of the pastor of a church: *First Lady of the church.*"

About the Title

It's My Prerogative ... the Lord gave me this title for the book. I'm keenly aware of the fact that *prerogative* may not be a word used every day by the average reader. In fact, it's often misused and mispelled. Still, the word holds deep meaning for me in relationship to my calling as First Lady of our church.

A *prerogative* is "a right," and some might think that it is a right either to reject or to accept this high calling, but I don't see it that way. A *prerogative* is also "a privilege," and that's the way I see it. I suppose that we could say a woman who is married to a man who becomes pastor of a church has the right to either reject or embrace her calling as First Lady, but I would say it this way: why would anyone not accept this great privilege? For my part, I say, "Yes, Lord! Yes! I will follow You!"

Foreword

In a society that has pills for spills, thrills and ills or a prescription for almost everything, very little is available to help the women who are struggling through the challenges of being a pastor's wife. They are expected to be women of perfection at all times and rarely given room to be women of creation, normal human beings. This book will help to bridge the gap between being a woman, a wife, a mother and the First Lady of a church.

Congratulations, Honey! You go, Girl!

Much Love!
Pastor Leroy J. Woodard, Jr.
Senior Pastor, CRM City Fellowship
One church with multiple locations

Introduction

I was compelled to write this book to encourage and empower those who, like me, suddenly find themselves in the seemingly untenable position of having to step up and assume the role of First Lady of a church with very little practical preparation for the ministry. We were living a fairly normal life, minding our own business and having to deal with the issues we all face on a day-to-day basis, when suddenly and unexpectedly, a whole new set of issues was dumped on us.

Although we had our own struggles in life, we were expected to be an example for everyone else to follow. Suddenly, every detail of our lives—how we dressed, the way we walked, the way we talked, how we treated others and every other detail of public (and, sometimes, private) life—came under severe scrutiny. Our children, who had enough problems already, were suddenly expected by everyone to be perfect, and everyone in the church felt empowered to correct them when they deemed their behavior to be anything but exemplary. They, too, were now considered to be representatives of the church and examples to all.

Suddenly, although we may have been considered laypersons in the church for years, we were expected to pick up any number of mantles of ministry. Some expected us to teach and preach instantly, and others expected us to lead traditional women's ministries—whether or not we seemed suited for those particular ministries. It was all very confusing and disorienting, and usually we had difficulty finding anyone to guide us.

What exactly does the First Lady of a church do? How can she cope with all of the added responsibilities laid on top of all of her already-existing responsibilities as wife, mother and professional in the community. It's mind boggling—to say the least.

One thing we know: as Christian ladies, our role is always to stand by our man, but now that phrase takes on new significance. Our man is no longer just a member of the church or just one of many ministers in a given congregation. Suddenly, he is the man of the hour, and everyone is looking to him for guidance. We know this man better than anyone else, including all of his weaknesses and failures, and we wonder, at times if he (or even the two of us together) are capable of taking on the huge assignment that has come our way.

But in a very real sense, it's too late for all of that. We're in. We're appointed. It's a done deal. We have no choice in the matter. Our only choice now is how we will react to what has become the new reality of our lives.

When I found myself in this extremely difficult position, there were few to whom I could turn for guidance. Who could teach me what to do or how to do it? After all, what does the average churchgoing Christian know about being the First Lady of the church? It goes without saying that I struggled for months and years as I learned.

But that was then, and this is now. I've now been a first lady for twelve years, and during that time, I've learned so much. I've learned to accept my circumstances and adapt to them. My husband helped me, but most of what I learned came from the Holy Spirit.

Now I want to share with others what I have been blessed to learn. I would not want to minimize in any way the struggles every first lady must face—especially in the early years of her ministry, but I firmly believe that if you can lay hold of the simple truths that I will outline in the pages of this book, you can be a great first lady.

Lady Gayle Woodard
Houston, Texas

Part I

*The Foundations of
Our High Calling*

Chapter One

Do I Even Want to Be the First Lady?

I praise you because I am fearfully and wonderfully made; your works are wonderful,
I know that full well.   Psalm 139:14

One day you wake up, and it seems to be a normal day, but then, before the day is over, your life has been turned upside down. Suddenly, your time is not your own, and everyone seems to have their own preconceived idea of what you should do and how you should do it. Now, instead of having to worry and care for one husband and a few children (responsibility enough for most of us in this modern world), you now have dozens or even hundreds (or sometimes thousands) of spiritual children, all with their specific and vital needs, and all of them seem to be competing for your attention. As the reality of all of this floods in upon you, your heart cries out: "I didn't ask for this! Do I even want to be the First Lady?"

A Job Nobody Chooses

Let's face it, this is not a job that anyone chooses. It can't be chosen. We didn't ask for it and, in some cases, we didn't want it, but we had no choice in the matter. We're married to a man who has a call of God upon his life, and he was chosen as pastor of the church. That automatically makes us the First Lady, and there's not much we can do about it.

But we do have another choice. We can either allow this moment to destroy us (and possibly destroy our spouse, our family and our church with us), or we can accept this call and learn to deal with it in a way that is pleasing to God. Some choose to live somewhere between those two points, and their life becomes miserable in the process.

Because the position of First Lady is seemingly forced upon us, many women rebel. They didn't ask for this, and so they refuse to accept it. They may feel compelled to keep the title. Most of us like the title. But that's all some want. They don't want to be an example for anyone else. They don't want to live in a fish bowl, constantly being scrutinized, analyzed and criticized. They don't want to be tied down with all the church activities. They don't want to take on any public ministry. They don't want other people coming to them with their problems. It's hard enough having to believe for the needs of a growing family, let alone having to believe for the needs of a growing church. But the title First Lady means something, something you cannot escape.

You, too, Are Called

Being a pastor's wife is an honor bestowed upon us by God Himself. He has appointed women of valor *"for such a time as this"* (Esther 4:14, KJV) just as much as He has appointed the men they fell in love with and married. He had a purpose in it all, and His purpose is fulfilled as we embrace His call and accept the challenges that it carries.

I love the Lord, and that's what made all the difference in me being given the respected position of First Lady. I felt honored by it, not burdened by it. I just wanted to be sure that I did my best to fulfill the trust God had placed in me, and I knew that to do that I would have to learn a lot.

When the Lord comes back, He won't call you First Lady. He'll call you by your given name. He knows you personally. He knew you before you were conceived. He knew you before you were born. He knew you before you gave your heart to Him. He knew you before you married. And He knew you before you became First Lady. And that's the basis of our calling—a personal relationship with the Creator of the Universe. We love Him, and He loves us, and somehow and for some reason, He chose to put us in this position. How can we not be grateful for such an honor? And how can we not embrace its challenge?

It was not my choice, but His, and yet my concern was not how I could avoid the heavy responsibilities of being First Lady, but how I could keep my heart in the right place, as I went about the task of learning to do what God had called me to do. Everything else must flow out of our calling. When any pastor's wife, or any minister's wife, for that matter, refuses to accept the call of God upon her life, that fact alone can make her husband's life a living Hell on earth. When we warmly embrace his call as our own, that makes all the difference.

If we can't get the call right, then forget all the other details of finding your place in the Church. Nothing will work for you—if you have not yet embraced the call!

What Will Really Matter in Eternity

When we all stand before God one day, the most important thing will be if we are saved or not—regardless of who we happen to have married. Beyond that, there is a world of opportunity in God that many are missing out on because they have not been willing to accept His call. Yes, as a new first lady, I felt overwhelmed. It was a lot to learn in a short time, and I sometimes wondered if I was up to the task. But in the days, weeks, months and years to come, I learned. I adjusted. I came to know who I was in God. And I came to understand better how I could serve Him and be happy in that service.

I didn't resent having to be an example for others. I

wanted to be that example. My only concern was what to do and how to do it, and He taught me that because I was willing to embrace what came along with the title.

Yes, I was confused for a while. Everybody seemed to be telling me that I had to preach and teach, and that didn't seem to be my gift. So I just prayed and asked God for direction. He gave me peace to understand where the others were coming from, but He also gave me specific direction for my own life. And, along with it, He gave me the confidence I needed to be the lady He had called me to be: saved and filled with His Holy Spirit. I wanted my light to shine, and He wanted my light to shine, so I just needed to pray and ask Him for the answers I needed for my ministry calling.

God Has Always Known Your Future

Way back in the time of Jeremiah (about six hundred years before Christ was born), the Lord said:

For I know the thoughts that I think toward you, says the LORD, thoughts of peace and not of evil, to give you a future and a hope.
                                        Jeremiah 29:11, NKJ

God has long known His plan for your life. He had something wonderful He wanted you to do. He wanted you to be First Lady of a great congregation. Embrace your call, and rise to the occasion.

You May Be Full of Questions

New first ladies are, understandably, full of questions like these:

- "Where do I fit into the ministry?"
- "What exactly am I supposed to do?"
- "How can I find time for all of these new responsibilities and still maintain my marriage and my home?"
- "How can I be a wife, a mother, an office worker [or whatever your chosen profession is] and First Lady all at once?"

They're all good questions, and I want to answer them as well as I can in the coming chapters. Let me say, initially, that your first obligation is to stand beside your husband and support him totally in all that he is undertaking for the Lord. Secondly, you must join with your husband in prayer to receive guidance on the area of ministry in which you personally should lead. Whichever ministry this turns out to be will be something you are passionate about and will be happy doing. Then, through that ministry, God will develop the gifts He has already placed on the inside of you. And, as the Bible declares, these gifts will make room for you:

A man's gift makes room for him,
And brings him before great men.

Proverbs 18:16, NKJ

It won't happen overnight, but in time, God will develop and perfect you, as you exercise your gifts in ministry.

Other Skills You Will Need

In the ministry, possessing people skills is very important, but God can add to you whatever you happen to be lacking. Ask Him to give you wisdom, patience and direction when talking with members of your congregation. You must never be partial to one over another, and you must never discriminate. You must have a forgiving and non-judgmental heart and be able to get to know people without judging them. You must be loving and kind to everyone. God loves them all, so just let His love flow out through you.

In our work as first ladies, we encounter a wide range of personalities. The key to connecting with your congregation is opening your heart to love every single one of them. God drew you to Himself through His loving kindness, and it is His loving kindness manifested through you that will draw others:

With loving-kindness have I drawn thee.

Jeremiah 31:3, KJV

Everyone wants to feel loved and appreciated. Realistically speaking, in a large church, you may not be able to get to everyone. But when opportunities arise for you to communicate with your church family, make it a point to express your love and appreciation for them in any way you can. You must come to view your congregation as your spiritual sons and daughters and you as their spiritual mother. As with our natural families, all of our children have different personalities and qualities, but we love them just the same.

God has strategically placed us in our ministry to lift and encourage our people through His Word and our example, as we walk with Christ. God does not make mistakes, and He didn't make one when He chose you for this ministry.

The people you are called to reach may not always be kind to you as First Lady. Many have a tendency to treat us differently, simply because we're the pastor's wife. These people may be experiencing personal situations that they're processing and working through. Whatever the reason, we must love them—in spite of their unlovely disposition toward us.

A Ministry Unto Itself

Being a pastor's wife is a ministry unto itself, and we must constantly remind ourselves of that fact. We are not in this ministry to make best friends or to enrich ourselves at the expense of others. We're in it to minister to the lives of hurting and needy people. I know it doesn't feel good to always give love and not receive it in return, and you may ask yourself sometimes, "What's wrong? What have I done to these people?" It is possible that you haven't done anything wrong. You were just picked out to be picked on, and God knew you could handle it.

As we minister to people, we must keep in mind that some of them are still growing in Christ. We must be sensitive to them on their particular level and listen to the Holy Spirit within us, as He shows us how to meet their need. And, with it all, God will never put more on us than we're able to bear.

So do you really want to be a pastor's wife? Well, you have no choice in the matter. You have been appointed by God Almighty. A great and challenging task lies before you, but it will be very rewarding, and it's all for the glory of God.

If you can lay hold of this simple truth, you can be a great first lady.

⌒ Journal for Chapter 1 ⌒

SCRIPTURE:

"For I know the plans I have for you," declares the LORD, *"plans to prosper you and not to harm you, plans to give you hope and a future."*   Jeremiah 29:11

WORDS OF INSPIRATION:

Follow God and His Word, and He will direct you and equip you for the task for which you were ordained from the foundations of the earth.

REFLECTIONS:

_____

_____

_____

_____

_____

_____

_____

_____

Chapter Two

The Story Behind My Glory

And the God of all grace, who called you to his eternal glory in Christ, after you have suffered a little while, will himself restore you and make you strong, firm and steadfast.   1 Peter 5:10

I know that, to others, it may seem like first ladies "have it all going on," but the truth is that sometimes we're all dressed up on the outside but all "messed up" on the inside. We, too, have issues to face in life. They may be church issues, family issues or personal issues. Through my research with many other pastors' wives, I've learned that first ladies today have to deal with issues stemming from childhood, marital issues, career issues and domestic issues. And, for some, the list is even more extensive. I have my own list.

I Have My Own List

As a little girl, I endured a lot. I came from a family that was not as fortunate as others. Mom and Dad faced many financial challenges, and so we were often uprooted and moved from house to house. As the oldest daughter in the family, I was given many responsibilities. For example, I had to help get my younger brothers and sisters ready for school every day.

On top of attending school, I had domestic chores, including cooking and cleaning. I had my own homework to do, and I was expected to help the other children with theirs as well. Sometimes, when there wasn't enough lunch money to go around, I had to let them eat, and I would have to wait until I got home in the afternoon from school.

Worst of all, I was cut off from my childhood and didn't get a fair opportunity, like my other sisters and brothers, just to be a child. Instead, I was expected to help keep everything going, and as a result, I rarely had any time for myself. In retrospect, this self-sacrifice, even though it was personally costly at the time, was necessary, and if I had it to do all over again, I would. Family is everything, and no sacrifice is too great when it comes to their welfare.

As time progressed, the demands upon me only increased. There is much more that I could say, but I said this much only to show that I wasn't born with a silver spoon in my mouth. I had a hard childhood, but I'm a survivor.

Just because a woman holds the position of pastor's wife, the First Lady of a church, doesn't mean that her life was easy or is easy now, any more than it makes her better than others. Personally, I never feel greater esteem for myself than I do for others. God has placed me in this position to walk alongside of my husband in ministry, and therefore I'm on a divine assignment from God. That's all there is to it.

The Transition to Married Life

After I finished school, I lived on my own and worked two jobs to achieve the goals I had set for myself. As I was pursuing these career goals, I met my soulmate, and about a year later we married.

When I first met him, he was very active in his father's church (as choir director and head of the music department), but, amazingly, he was not yet saved. By the time we married, he had been saved, but he wasn't yet filled with the Spirit. He had a bad temper and had some serious growing up to do. After all the things I'd had to endure, I now found myself saying, "Here I go again, putting myself through more pain." But I was able to see great potential in him, so I stayed with him, praying for him and speaking into his life.

Before long, we had a baby boy, and I was reminded

of my duties in childhood. I was taking care of babies again, but now I was also working outside the home. My husband's commitments to the church kept him away often, and we began having marital and financial problems, and they both grew steadily worse.

I'll never forget the day I came home from work, and he told me that there was a power outage in the apartment complex where we lived. Later, I learned differently. He had been too embarrassed to tell me that our electricity had been disconnected because we hadn't been able to pay the bill. On top of that, we had written checks for pampers and milk for our infant son against an account that had no money in it. No, my life was not an easy one.

Time passed, our son grew, and it was now time for him to start school. Because of the problems his dad and I were having at home, our son faced several personal challenges. Our domestic disputes translated into academic struggles for him. These problems continued for years, and for years I prayed and prayed, and I cried and cried.

God Heard My Cries

In time, my husband was filled with the Spirit, God called him to the ministry, and I began to see the light of spiritual growth and maturity in him.

I never gave up on him. Through prayer and with the help of God, he changed. In time, God completely transformed him into a very loving, caring, giving person and an awesome teacher of the Word.

Now, after many years of marriage, we are the proud parents of two successful sons, Leroy Junior (L.J.), our eldest, who right now is a sophomore in college and Demond, our youngest, a junior in high school. They are now experiencing the fruits of a balanced and healthy family life. Those days of enduring hurts are over, and my husband now celebrates, exalts, respects, values and honors me as his wife, and he recognizes the benefit of my endurance and sacrifice.

Your Particular Case

Not every woman will be able to identify with these particular scenarios, but whatever your particular case, never give up on your husband—no matter what obstacles may come your way. Does not God's Word command us?:

What God has joined together, let not man [or circumstance] separate.　　Matthew 19:6, NKJ

Continue to pray for your husband, speak into his life and be an example to him, and in time, God will restore and renew him. Always remember, a sanctified wife sanctifies her husband:

For the unbelieving husband is sanctified by the wife,

and the unbelieving wife is sanctified by the husband:
else were your children unclean; but now are they holy.

1 Corinthians 7:14, KJV

My Husband Becomes a Pastor

Subsequent to my husband's salvation and the accep-
tance of his call to the ministry, his father, the late Bishop
L.J. Woodard, Sr., became ill. During his illness, my husband assisted him a great deal, because there were times
when his father didn't feel well enough to bear the load of
the ministry alone. Then, early one Sunday morning,
God called Bishop Woodard home. That was a difficult
day for me. My father-in-law had become very near and
dear to my heart, for he had treated me as though I were
his own daughter. May God rest his soul.

From that day forward, my husband became pastor of
the church and continued to build the ministry for which
Bishop Woodard had laid the foundation. Automatically
that placed me in the position of First Lady of the congregation. It was like the children's game, "Ready or not, you
shall be caught." Well, needless to say, I wasn't ready.
What was I supposed to do now?

I had a vague notion that being a first lady required a
woman to stand by her husband, but what did that really
mean? Being a pastor's wife was not something I had
ever desired, but there I was—ready or not. This could
have been a breaking point for me, but somehow I sensed

that God had a purpose in it all. He had a plan for our lives, and He wanted us to continue the ministry Bishop Woodard had started.

My story, of course, continues, and there are new challenges every day. But now we're in a totally different phase of our lives. It's harvest time, and I'm reaping the benefits of the years of tears and prayers I sowed.

What's your story? God's Word declares that He *"will himself restore you and make you strong, firm and stead-fast."* Believe Him for that.

If you can lay hold of this simple truth, you can be a great first lady.

Journal for Chapter 2

SCRIPTURE:

And the God of all grace, who called you to his eternal glory in Christ, after you have suffered a little while, will himself restore you and make you strong, firm and steadfast. 1 Peter 5:10

WORDS OF INSPIRATION:

What's your story? If you look carefully, you will surely see God's hand in it all, bringing you to this moment for this very purpose. Embrace His call upon your life.

REFLECTIONS:

_____

_____

_____

_____

_____

_____

_____

_____

_____

_____

_____

Chapter Three

It's All About Ministry

And whatever you do in word or deed, do all in the name of the Lord Jesus, giving thanks to God the Father through Him. Colossians 3:17, NKJ

When we accept the call of God upon our lives, something changes. From that moment on, life is not about us anymore. It's all about ministry.

We Now Have a Greater Purpose in Life

This doesn't mean that we stop living. We don't. It doesn't mean that we're not like other people. We are. What it does mean is that we now have a higher purpose in life, and that higher purpose takes precedence over most everything else. Most every decision we will make from this moment on is based on how it will affect the ministry God has entrusted into our hands. And that's the way it has to be.

God has chosen and anointed us to serve and feed and lead His people, and it's all for His glory, not our own. Ministry therefore is not a burden; it's a wonderful opportunity. We can now serve and mentor and counsel others and see their lives enhanced as a result. As teachers, pastors and bishops, we are on a divine assignment from God, and it's difficult to put into words the wonderful feeling we have when we see the power of God moving through us into the lives of other people. God literally changes them through the Word we minister.

One of my favorite personal mottos for ministry is this: "You won't leave the way you came, in Jesus' name." I see people coming in and joining the church, and they're one way. Then, as time goes on, I see them grow in the Word, and I can notice a different look about them and a different walk. They're now happy in themselves and also beginning to minister to others. What could be more wonderful than that?

Ministry Is Not Limited to the Four Walls of the Church

But our ministry is not limited to the four walls of the church. It goes far beyond. We're called to go out and reach the unreachable in our communities and also in other communities. We're called to go anywhere and everywhere that people are hungering for righteousness. Jesus said:

*Blessed are they which do hunger and thirst after right-
eousness for they shall be filled.* Matthew 5:6, KJV

We have the privilege of interceding for God's answer to the people's prayer. As they seek Him, He will give them what they're hungering and thirsting for. What a great privilege that is! And it changes everything.

Sometimes, when we go out, we're honored and served as Pastor and First Lady, but it is an even greater privilege for us to be the ones who do the serving. This calling is so vital that we must guard against getting so caught up in a leadership role that we forget the importance of serving and neglect to do it. God has placed an awesome responsibility into our hands, and the fact that He chose us shows that He is trusting us and depending upon us to fulfill our divine assignment.

Ministry Can Take You Around the World

Sometimes ministry can take you around the world. Even if we don't happen to have a ministry of preaching and teaching, our husbands are called upon to minister to people in other states and other countries, and we, as first ladies, must be prepared to assist them when they need us. It's always very exciting for me when I'm able to travel with my husband and see different people and places and know that we're all working together toward the same goal. Praising and worshipping God together and then seeing His power at work through the ministry He manifests is wonderful. Seeing people being delivered and set free from the enemy's attack is a joy—wherever it happens to take place!

So, first ladies, have some bags packed and be ready for ministry at all times, for God has much more for you to do. There are many lives that will be saved through you in the days to come.

When you travel, don't forget to pack a special bag containing items to assist your husband in ministry. Learn what he needs when he travels and have it handy for him. Don't forget your most important weapon, which is your Bible. This will assure that you'll always be prepared to walk in your assignment when the moment of opportunity arrives.

And never forget what a privilege it is to serve. Instead of complaining about your responsibilities, recognize each day how blessed you are to be a pastor's wife.

If you can lay hold of this simple truth, you can be a great first lady.

Journal for Chapter 3

SCRIPTURE:

And whatever you do, whether in word or deed, do it all in the name of the Lord Jesus, giving thanks to God the Father through Him. Colossians 3:17

WORDS OF INSPIRATION:

Continuing to seek God's righteousness, for you, means focusing on ministry, for this is your calling. Count it a great privilege. It can take you around the world and cause you to be a blessing to people everywhere.

REFLECTIONS:

_____

_____

_____

_____

_____

_____

_____

_____

_____

Part II

What's a First Lady Like?

Chapter Four

The Character of a First Lady

Who can find a virtuous woman? for her price is far above rubies. Proverbs 31:10, KJV

Everyone has high expectations for a first lady. Her character must be of the highest quality. This fact can be daunting for those who are suddenly thrust into such a demanding role. Always remember, however, that we all feel unworthy in such a position, and that we have the Lord we can call on to help us at every step of the process.

What Is a First Lady Like?

The character of a first lady should always be graceful, yet humble, assertive, but not boastful. She should always carry herself like a lady. Docile and delicate, yet strong, she should be kind and polite.

She looks upon everyone with love. She never sees color or gender. She is positive, optimistic and confident, and she sees the good in people. In short, she embodies the virtues of Proverbs 31, and she always represents well the women of her congregation through her character.

A first lady monitors her speech, and is *"slow to speak"* (James 1:19, NKJ). Before she speaks, she listens so that she can learn, and therefore when she does speak, she speaks with wisdom and not foolishly.

Because of this trait, her husband trusts her character and is confident that she will bring him honor and not shame, good and not evil, for she is, first and foremost, a woman who fears the Lord. Having such a woman by his side is very important to the success of any pastor. According to Proverbs:

> *An excellent wife is the crown of her husband,*
> *But she who causes shame is like rottenness in his*
> *bones.*   Proverbs 12:4, NKJ

You Are a Representative

There are times when a pastor and his wife may not be in agreement and are having some family problem, but this fact should never become obvious to the other members of the congregation. While we're preparing our bodies for worship service, we should pray that the Lord prepares our spirits as well, so that we will not, in any way, hinder the service or bring shame to our husbands or to the church.

But always remember that your character also represents you individually as a godly woman. You shouldn't desire to exude good character only for the sake of the church or only when you're in service. Nor should you do it just for your husband's sake. You should do it primarily for yourself. You should always desire to be a professional woman who walks in integrity and excellence and brings glory to God.

Your character always compliments your true essence, so walk with your head up, First Lady, and know who you are in God. You are somebody; you are a blessing to your husband, your children and the congregation.

Your character speaks volumes to the people you meet in your workplace or wherever you happen to go. So, let it shine. You are God's queen. Everyone who comes in contact with you should see your light shining. You represent your husband, your family and your church. But more than anything, you represent your Lord and Savior Jesus Christ, so do it with style.

When you walk into a room, your character should precede you. The very atmosphere in that room should feel the love and the kindness of your spirit. You possess the power to shift a bad environment into one that is very pleasant, because of the Holy Spirit that is within you. So continue to put on the character of a queen and remember who you are and Whose you are and that God loves you.

If you can lay hold of this simple truth, you can be a great first lady.

Journal for Chapter 4

SCRIPTURE:

An excellent wife is the crown of her husband,
But she who causes shame is like rottenness in his
bones.   Proverbs 12:4, NKJ

WORDS OF INSPIRATION:

Your beautiful character will take you before nobles
and royalty, so continue to put on the character of a
queen.

REFLECTIONS:

_____

_____

_____

_____

_____

_____

_____

_____

_____

_____

Chapter Five

The Ministry of a First Lady

There are different kinds of gifts, but the same Spirit.
There are different kinds of service, but the same Lord.
There are different kinds of working, but the same God
works all of them in all men. Now to each one the
manifestation of the Spirit is given for the common
good.   1 Corinthians 12:4-7

For a first lady, finding your place in the ministry is sometimes not an easy task, and it may not happen overnight. You already know that you're called to be your husband's wife, his helpmeet, and to work alongside him in ministry. You may not be confident of your own leadership position in other areas of ministry, unless you were already in leadership before you were married. You must now take time to discover how God has shaped you to lead and what specific ministry He has in mind for you.

Finding Your Place

There are several ways to find your place. You can start by seeking God about your specific spiritual gifts. It is clear from Paul's letter to the Corinthians that there are many different gifts and many different ministries in the Church. We were not all cut from the same mold, and to think that each of us must fit the same spot would be a mistake.

There are clearly many different needs within a given church, and this necessitates many varied ministries. Your particular area of service should be driven by your personal passions. God placed those desires within you, and He did that so that you would serve Him in some specific area of life.

This variety of desire and gifting does not make one either more or less than someone else, only different. There may be a variety of gifts and ministries, but they're all from the same God who is working in all our lives. Some specific spiritual gift has been given to each of us, and it is for the purpose of helping the entire Church.

Discover Your Passion

So you must discover your passion. Do you love to work with young children or with teens? Do you have a heart for unwed mothers or for the homeless? What do you enjoy doing? What would you do even without receiving any reward?

Think about your personality type. Are you an introvert? An extrovert? A dreamer? A detail person?

Also think about your personal life and the experiences you've had that might prove helpful to someone else. Sometimes this is all part of the process. Why is all of this so important? You will only be content in your role as a pastor's or minister's wife if you yourself are operating in your true divine calling.

You Are Not Alone

Remember this too! You are not alone. We can rejoice and be glad that we have a heavenly Father who not only loves us, but who also will never leave us alone. He's "got our back." He has promised:

> *Be strong and courageous. Do not be afraid or terrified because of them, for the LORD your God goes with you; he will never leave you nor forsake you.*
>
> Deuteronomy 31:6

God has creatively custom-tailored you for your specific role in ministry. Therefore it's okay if you don't always feel as though you fit into the traditional role of pastor's or minister's wife. Be confident in who you are as First Lady and as an individual minister in the Body of Christ.

Unto Whom Is Our Ministry?

Finally, always remember unto whom you are rendering your services. Your ministry is unto God first, not unto your husband, your children, your relatives, your congregation or your community. It is Him you must please more than any other. So remain focused, and stay the course, and God will honor your faithfulness. In this, be encouraged.

If you can lay hold of this simple truth, you can be a great first lady.

Journal for Chapter 5

SCRIPTURE:

There are different kinds of spiritual gifts, but it is the same Holy Spirit who is the source of them all.

1 Corinthians 12:4, NLT

WORDS OF INSPIRATION:

God's Word tells us not to try to compare ourselves with what He has given someone else. Be confident in what He has put in you and who He created you to be. We are all different, but God uses our individual gifts to work together for the common good.

REFLECTIONS:

_____

_____

_____

_____

_____

_____

_____

_____

Chapter Six

The Dress of a First Lady

I also want women to dress modestly, with decency and propriety, not with braided hair or gold or pearls or expensive clothes, but with good deeds, appropriate for women who profess to worship God.

1 Timothy 2:9-10

It should be that of your inner self, the unfading beauty of a gentle and quiet spirit, which is of great worth in God's sight.
1 Peter 3:4

Although there are few hard and fast rules about how first ladies must dress, there are some important guidelines to follow, and we must begin with what the Bible specifically says is God's will for all women who profess to love Him. They are *"to dress modestly, with decency and propriety."* That seems to be self-explanatory. Our emphasis, as godly women, must not be only on the exterior.

The interior must get equal and prior attention. God is looking to find in us *"the unfading beauty of a gentle and quiet spirit."* Who could say it better than that?

A first lady, therefore, must dress appropriately for her high calling, and she will not wear clothes that only draw attention to herself. Instead of relying on her clothes, she must possess a beauty of her own, one that comes from within her spirit.

It's Okay to Wear Stylish Clothes

Does this mean that we cannot wear stylish or beautiful clothes? Of course not. Many first ladies probably have some St. John, Tahari, Dana, Chanel and Donna Karan brand clothes in their closet, and there's nothing wrong with possessing the finer things of life—including designer clothes, shoes and bags. After all, our Father not only owns the cattle on a thousand hills; He owns the hills on which the cattle graze. If He can clothe the lilies of the field, then how much more will He take care of His own children? You are heirs to His kingdom and abundance is your birthright. Adorn yourself accordingly, for you are examples that others will follow.

What does it say to the members of your congregation about God when you come to church week after week wearing the same drab clothing? Are you a good representation of the Father's will? Do you represent your husband well? Do you represent the church well? Let God be glorified in all that you do.

That said, material possessions must never be allowed to define you. They can identify who you are, but they must simply enhance your already-present beauty. If everything you wear follows God's guidelines and pleases Him, then who can criticize it? It's usually easy to spot a virtuous woman, and that's the image a first lady always wants to put forth.

We Must Be More than Dress

Of course, if all we have is the appropriate dress and there's nothing to back it up, that's not good either. A first lady needs wisdom, discernment and insight, and you can't buy these at a fine clothing store. She must be submissive to her husband, and that's not for sale at any price.

One of the most important considerations any first lady should think of is her responsibility as a leader and an example to the other women of the church. She is a teacher, and she teaches first by her actions and secondly by her words. She is concerned for the welfare of all others and thinks of them before herself, and this fact is reflected in her appearance.

Modest and yet stylish, neither bold nor assertive, appealing and picturesque when she represents her man ... it's not an easy balance for a first lady to reach, but ask God to help you.

If you can lay hold of this simple truth, you can be a great first lady.

Journal for Chapter 6

SCRIPTURE:

I also want women to dress modestly, with decency and propriety, not with braided hair or gold or pearls or expensive clothes, but with good deeds, appropriate for women who profess to worship God.

1 Timothy 2:9-10

WORDS OF INSPIRATION:

Remember, the attire of a first lady is not always the shimmering, sparkling and extravagant attire we might expect. First of all, a first lady must be adorned with modesty, humility and virtue.

REFLECTIONS:

_____

_____

_____

_____

_____

_____

_____

_____

_____

Chapter Seven

The Shoes of a First Lady

Let us not become weary in doing good, for at the proper time we will reap a harvest if we do not give up.

Galatians 6:9

For shoes, put on the peace that comes from the Good News, so that you will be fully prepared.

Ephesians 6:15, NLT

The walk of a first lady is not an easy one, and this is sometimes literal as well as figurative. Take a look at my shoes, and you'll know what I mean by this.

My Shoes Get All Scarred Up

My shoes get all scarred up, the heels get tattered, and the soles are often worn, and it's no wonder, for there are so many special church conferences, revivals and other meetings to attend. There are airports to traverse and planes to board. As a result, sometimes my feet are tired and hurting, and yet I must go on. That's what ministry is all about.

There are late meetings, early morning prayers, early wake-up calls, going without for the sake of others, walking alone sometimes and walking in places I really don't even want to be. But because of the shoes I wear, I must go on.

Sometimes I have to walk in dark places, where I can't see well, but I trust that God sees and knows all. Sometimes I have to enter environments where I'm really not welcomed, but because of the shoes I wear, I go. Sometimes I'm forced to go into businesses I'm unfamiliar with, but because of the shoes I wear, I go.

My walk not only has to take into account the ministry responsibilities, but also my responsibilities to my husband, my children, my family, my friends and my community. That's a lot of walking. No wonder my feet get tired!

A Lot of Steps to Take

As a first lady, I not only have a lot of steps to take. I also have to walk with my head up high—even when I'm feeling down. The shoes that I wear require it. I'm walking in faith. I'm walking in God's strength. I go on for Him and because of Him.

I sometimes say to the Lord, "I need some new shoes, for these are so worn," but He answers, "I made these shoes just for you, and there's only one pair of them. They're unique in all the earth, and no one else could wear them but you." So I go on because of the shoes I wear.

Actually, my shoes are beautiful, and they look inviting to others, but others just don't know how badly my feet hurt at times. These are not easy shoes to wear.

But there's also something magical about these shoes. When my body and spirit are downtrodden, my shoes continue to travel: to hospital visits, private counseling and other special meetings. I must go, and my shoes take me anyway.

The Journey Called Ministry

This journey called ministry is not an easy one, but I understand that God has ordained and appointed me for it, and so I make it with joy. He will continue to guide and direct my paths and give me the strength I need to continue on. I'm sure of it.

Each week, my shoes take me to all three of our church's locations, almost an hour apart. When we get to each location, there are many people there with needs to be ministered to and many souls to be won for Christ. So

I continue to walk in the ministry alongside my husband, my shoes serving me at their fullest capacity.

Walking by my husband's side to many places is a great honor. I will have to admit that I do get tired sometimes *in* ministry, but I've never gotten tired *of* ministry. As a first lady, we have to wear some special shoes because we have so many places to go.

Ministry calls for service, and we must be ready and willing at all times to say, "Lord, whatever You want me to do and wherever You want me to go, I'll say yes." My shoes will take me there.

My Favorite Shoes

My favorite shoes are spiritual. I go to my secret closet, the Holy of Holies, and there I petition God for my spiritual life, so that He can direct me on the right path and help me put on my spiritual shoes. Wearing them is not always easy, and sometimes I need Him to adjust the fit. Whether it's my sandals of salvation, my heels of humility or my flip-flops of faith, He continues to give me the strength and direction, no matter what fit or style may be required. I have to be ready and stay prepared for whatever it is He directs me to do, and that's why it's so important that I hear from Him daily.

When it comes time to intercede for my husband and children, for our ministry, for the members of our church and for myself, I must then put on my boots of spiritual warfare. As I pray for others, I encourage and lift them up through the Word of God. My spiritual shoes are full of God's anointed power, and He has definitely appointed me to the ministry He placed within my spirit.

The shoes that God has given me are worn with passion, respect, wisdom and guidance. I feel deeply honored that He has chosen me to wear such beautiful and graceful shoes, shoes that we know will never wear out. These shoes were given to me by our Lord and Savior, Jesus Christ Himself. Put on your spiritual shoes and learn the walk of a first lady.

If you can lay hold of this simple truth, you can be a great first lady.

Journal for Chapter 7

SCRIPTURE:

Let us not become weary in doing good, for at the proper time we will reap a harvest if we do not give up.

Galatians 6:9

WORDS OF INSPIRATION:

No one but you can walk in the special shoes you've received from God Almighty.

REFLECTIONS:

_____

_____

_____

_____

_____

_____

_____

_____

_____

_____

_____

_____

Chapter Eight

The Fragrance of a First Lady

I arose to open to my beloved;
And my hands dripped with myrrh,
My fingers with liquid myrrh,
On the handles of the lock.

Song of Solomon 5:5, NKJ

There's one common language that all women everywhere share, and that's the language of smelling good. A first lady must have this department down to a science.

Freshness for Ministry

First ladies are very involved in ministry, and they have many other responsibilities. They're very busy women, but they must never be too busy to remember how to take care of their personal hygiene.

For you that are new to this elite calling of first ladies, this is extremely important. It may not seem like this should even have to be discussed, but how you smell has a direct impact on whether or not you will have effective ministry. So please take heed. The following paragraphs will explain why this is such an integral part of successful ministry.

Staying on the Go

A first lady stays on the go. She's ministering, along with her husband, and they may spend many hours a day in worship or seeking to save lost souls. For the first lady, it's imperative that personal hygiene become a priority because her husband relies on her heavily, and so she must always be prepared. He may ask her to lay hands on someone and pray for them. For this purpose, keep a breath mint in your possession at all times.

You may also want to carry a change of clothing with you, for you may perspire at some point and need to freshen up. At the very least, your bag should contain the following: wet ones, perfume, fresh pantyhose, a comb, a brush, dental floss, toothpaste, a toothbrush and, of course, your makeup bag.

Extend Your Good Hygiene to Your Intimate Times

After a long day serving and saving souls, it's time for you and your husband to relax and retire for the day.

Even then, your need to smell good does not end. Always have a variety of his favorite perfumes on hand. Some favorites might include: Coco Chanel, Prada and Dolce & Gabana and after-bath lotions such as Victoria Secret or Bath & Body Works. Your man pays attention to these details, so this is another level of ministry, ladies. When you pay attention to these details, you're ministering to him, and that's an important ministry.

Being Fresh for Him

Along with his favorite perfumes, have his favorite lingerie ready. You can always tell which one is his favorite because he asks you to wear it on special occasions.

Ministering in tandem to others and then enjoying one another after ministry is completed should both be void of personal hygiene issues. Just remember to always be conscious of this all-important issue.

Personal hygiene includes your outer appearance as well. A first lady's closet should reflect cleanliness. It should always be neat and appealing. Your clothing should always be clean and ironed or steamed by the cleaners. First ladies must always look and smell their best because they're always being watched and mimicked.

If you can lay hold of this simple truth, you can be a great first lady.

⌢ Journal for Chapter 8 ⌢

SCRIPTURE:

I arose to open for my beloved,
And my hands dripped with myrrh,
My fingers with liquid myrrh,
On the handles of the lock.

Song of Solomon 5:5, NKJ

WORDS OF INSPIRATION:

As women, we must never be negligent about the way we look and smell. Always be very careful with your cleanliness and your appearance. Remember, everyone is watching. You are a representative of the Almighty.

REFLECTIONS:

_____

_____

_____

_____

_____

_____

_____

_____

Chapter Nine

The Finances of a First Lady

Keep your lives free from the love of money and be content with what you have, because God has said, "Never will I leave you; never will I forsake you."

Hebrews 13:5

The finances of a first lady are complicated by the fact that she and her husband have now taken upon themselves many of the burdens of the ministry, on top of the existing burden they already bear for their own family. And, for Americans in the twenty-first century, nothing is simple about finances.

Keeping Up with the Joneses

The lives of a great majority of Americans today are complicated by the constant pressure to keep up with *the*

Joneses. Who are *the Joneses* anyway? And why should they have anything to say about how we live or what we buy or wear?

Historically speaking, the expression "keeping up with *the Joneses*," got its start in 1913 as the title of a comic strip. The strip detailed the lives of two families: *the McGinnises* and *the Joneses*. *The McGinnises* were always envious of *the Joneses* and therefore were constantly struggling to have as much or more than *the Joneses* had. That comic strip gave rise to a new expression, one that has brought a curse upon many Americans.

The New Dictionary of Cultural Literacy gives the definition of this phrase, *keeping up with* the Joneses, as "striving to achieve or own as much as the people around you" (New York, NY, Houghton Mifflin Company; Hirsch, E.D, Kett, Joseph F. and Trefil, James: 2002). If you want to keep up with *the Joneses* in your neighborhood, you may have to own at least three automobiles. Thus, the proverbial *Joneses* have set the pace for all of us, and what's amazing is that no one I know has ever yet met them.

Owning a big new house and new cars, just to keep up with *the Joneses,* is very foolish and just might put you "in the poor house." God's Word teaches us not to be controlled by money or things. We're not only commanded not to love money, but we're also commanded: *"be content with what you have."*

Twenty-First Century Pressures

That thought seems to be far from the minds of most Christians today. Modern advertising constantly tries to remind us of how much better our lives could be if only we had the latest and best gadget, vehicle, house or clothes. Our focus, as believers, should be God Himself. We don't have to worry about keeping up with the Joneses because our God promised, *"Never will I leave you; never will I forsake you."* God has a plan for you, and His plan for others is not the same. So they may not need what you have, and you probably don't need what they have.

Constantly trying to keep up with the Joneses will only create envy and jealousy, which can have disastrous results. Just look at what happened when Cain envied Abel, Joseph's brothers envied him and King Saul suddenly envied the young David. These are all good examples of why we must never allow the enemy to deceive us through the spirit of envy or the love of money and power.

In Practical Terms

What does this mean to us in practical terms? It means that we must learn to budget and then manage the finances God makes available to us, and we must live life at our own pace—not someone else's. For instance, you may need to upgrade your transportation situation because the car you have is on its last leg, but that doesn't mean that you have to outdo your neighbor by buying a Cadillac Escalade, when you can't realistically afford it. Have you ever stopped to think that maybe the reason your neighbors bought an Escalade is that they have a larger family?

Trying to keep up with the Joneses will make you spend unnecessary time and money that could be allocated to something that would be more beneficial to you and your family. By budgeting your finances and setting attainable goals, you can eliminate the stress of always needing to have more than you actually receive. In America today, nothing is ever enough, and that can't be right. Many who have large incomes are still deeply in debt. Does that even make good sense?

Don't Be Afraid to Talk About Money

Some Christians feel uncomfortable talking about money, but the Bible talks about it a lot. It shows how money can be managed profitably. There are several wealth-building strategies that you can implement in your life today that will establish wealth for your family for generations to come. These don't necessarily require large new sources of income. Here are some practical ideas you might want to consider.

Marketing your hobbies and utilizing your professional skills both have the power to generate additional income for you. God has already equipped you with the tools you need to build and access your reservoir of wealth. Now you must position yourself to take advantage of opportunities that come your way. Learn to save, invest and generate several different streams of income. Surprisingly, some of these can be small. God will always open a door of opportunity, but are you looking for it?

God has already provided all the resources we need to complete our divine purpose and realize our divine blessings. Learning to manage and budget your own finances will position you to *be* the Joneses instead of trying to keep up with them. God has already equipped and prepared us. We must now take our rightful place in the prosperity He has said is rightfully ours.

Seek Professional Guidance

As you seek to build wealth for your family and your ministry, I recommend that you access as many reputable resources as you can to gain more knowledge. There are standard principles that govern wealth acquisition. Having an expert that is knowledgeable, such as a financial consultant, will help you initiate and maintain your financial plans. Here's a list of online resources you might also find helpful:

- www.usaa.com
- www.dinkytown.com

- your local bank
- www.christianadvice .net
   /the_bible_on_money.htm
- www.forbes.com
- money.cnn.com
- www.kidsmoney.org
- www.younginvestor.com
- www.kids.gov/k_money.htm

It won't happen for you automatically; you have to make it happen. And God will be there to help you every step of the way, for His will is that you prosper.

If you can lay hold of this simple truth, you can be a great first lady.

---

* Web sites change frequently. If these particular ones are not available, use your web browser to find others that are.

Journal for Chapter 9

SCRIPTURE:

Keep your lives free from the love of money and be content with what you have, because God has said, "Never will I leave you; never will I forsake you."

Hebrews 13:5

WORDS OF INSPIRATION:

If we can remember that God's Spirit in us makes us powerful, there can be limitless opportunity for us to make manifest God's glory in our lives. Let us believe that we are brilliant, talented, fabulous and loving, for these fruits are always in season and within our reach.

REFLECTIONS:

Part III

Making Time
for What's Important

Chapter Ten

Making Time for God

Call to me and I will answer you and tell you great and unsearchable things you do not know.

Jeremiah 33:3

As strange as it may seem, many of those who are called to ministry become so busy that they actually neglect God and fail to spend enough quality time with Him. What a mistake that is! It is God who calls us, and only He can empower us on a daily basis to fulfill our calling.

There are many time constraints in ministry. And just because we're now in ministry, this never gives us the right to neglect our families, so we have a lot of responsibilities, and yet there are still only twenty-four hours in every day. This means that we have to set priorities when it comes to our time. And God always has to come first. How can it be any other way? Talking to God is a matter of life and death. This is true for every believer, but it is even more true for those in ministry.

Prayer Is Communication with God

Prayer is communication with God, and you need to talk to Him. He has put principles and policies into place to help us with every situation of life. If you are dealing with difficult children, God has a way for you to cope with those children. You may be facing a crisis within your ministry. Well, God has the answer for overcoming that difficulty. Whatever it is that you need today, if you will seek the face of God through prayer, He has an answer for you. He said, just *"call,"* and He promised, *"I will answer."* What a powerful promise!

God has given us authority over everything that troubles us, and through prayer, we can actually change the outcome of the enemy's plans for our lives:

> *I have given you authority to trample on snakes and scorpions and to overcome all the power of the enemy; nothing will harm you.* Luke 10:19

When I became the First Lady of our church, I knew from the beginning that I needed to pray, but I had other questions: How often should I pray? And how exactly should I pray? The answer soon became obvious. I should be talking to God every day about small issues, just as I also prayed about the seemingly insurmountable problems. If I trust Him, He has promised never to fail me:

> *Trust in the LORD with all your heart and lean not unto your own understanding; in all your ways acknowledge him, and he will make your paths straight.*   Proverbs 3:5-6

God Doesn't Need the Prayer; You Do

It's not God who needs the prayer; it's you. He already knows all about you, but when you spend time with Him in prayer, you become more intimate with Him. You begin to understand His character more. Your daily conversation is then anchored in the truth of His character, His faithful love, His total forgiveness and His tenderness.

When you spend time with God, you grow closer to Him, and you know what is pleasing to Him. Then you will find that God is just waiting to bless you in ways that you could never have imagined before. For instance, He will give you true peace and hope.

Does God Always Answer?

This led me to another question, "Does God always answer my prayer?" I came to the conclusion that He does, but sometimes we're just not listening when He gives us the answer.

Sometimes we want the answer right now, and God is telling us to wait. Sometimes His answer is "not now" and can even be "no" because we don't always pray His perfect will. At other times, He says to us, "Yes, help is on the way." I have learned that, when I have prayed, I must then be still to hear exactly what God is saying to me about my concern.

Something Positive Happens Every Day

My experience is that when I pray something positive happens every day. My heart has become softer toward God and now, instead of seeing things through eyes of hopelessness, I know that there's hope for every situation. God can restore people and situations that have been destroyed and devoured. He said:

> *I will repay you for the years the locusts have eaten—*
> *the great locust and the young locust, the other locusts*
> *and the locust swarm—my great army that I sent*
> *among you.* Joel 2:25

Pray God's Word

I have also learned to pray God's Word. When I pray what He has declared to be His will, it is manifested here on earth. His Word is powerful:

For the word of God is quick, and powerful, and sharper than any two-edged sword.   Hebrews 4:12, KJV

I have discovered that I cannot pray selfish prayers and expect results. I've also learned that when I ask God to fulfill His will in my life, my needs, wants and desires were immediately met. At first, this was very difficult for me to understand. However, as I continued to seek the face of God, my understanding increased. Now, instead of praying and asking God to supply all *my needs*, I pray and ask Him to fulfill *His will*. I know that consequently God's will in my life and the lives of those for whom I have prayed will be fulfilled. The apostle John taught the early Church:

This is the confidence we have in approaching God: that if we ask anything according to his will, he hears us.   1 John 5:14

Along with prayer, we must also spend other quality time with God. This could be through meditating on His Word, the reading of the Bible. (More on this in the following chapter.) This is what I call "face time," and all of us need more of it.

Sometimes we need to just be quiet and let the Holy Spirit speak to us. Just as we make time for our family and friends, we must also make time for God. The more time we spend with our family and friends, the closer the relationship develops, and it's the same with God. We need time to look at nature and reflect on all the wonderful things He has created, but we have to make up our minds to set aside time that will be only for God.

In this hectic world, with our busy life-styles, it's easy to get so enmeshed in other responsibilities that we never make time for God. Some of us may spend a couple of hours a week attending church or Bible study, but then the routines of life and the infamous rat race catches up with us. We find ourselves focusing on other cares, and we forget about our prior commitment to "face time" with God. With stress-inducing circumstances like health issues, career and family situations, the necessity to bask in the presence of our mighty Father in Heaven has never been more important.

This "face time" with God allows us to truly get to know Him, to fellowship with Him and to steal away from the worries and cares of this world. When Moses spent time with God, his face became radiant:

> *But whenever he entered the LORD's presence to speak with him, he removed the veil until he came out. And when he came out and told the Israelites what he had been commanded, they saw that his face was radiant.*
> Exodus 34:34

Spending quality time with God will always pay off!

If you can lay hold of this simple truth, you can be a great first lady.

Journal for Chapter 10

SCRIPTURE:

Call to me and I will answer you and tell you great and unsearchable things you do not know.

Jeremiah 33:3

WORDS OF INSPIRATION:

God hears and honors your prayer, so continue to get in that quiet place with Him. There's power in fasting and praying, and when you do it, change is sure to come.

REFLECTIONS:

_____

_____

_____

_____

_____

_____

_____

_____

_____

_____

Chapter Eleven

Making Time for His Word

Be diligent to present yourself approved to God, a worker who does not need to be ashamed, rightly dividing the word of truth.   2 Timothy 2:15, NKJ

As children of the King and chosen instruments for the advancement of His Kingdom, we must each one *"study to show [ourselves] approved"* (KJV). The work that we are called to is not our own. We are leading God's people, preaching His Word and doing His work. Therefore we must have His Word in our hearts, so that we can do things His way. To neglect the Word of God is tantamount to cutting off our Source of life. Therefore, we must always make time for His Word.

The Word Keeps Us Strong

It is the Word of God that keeps us strong and courageous, and it fits every circumstance we may face in our daily lives. God has something to say to help and guide you through your current crisis or need—whatever it might be.

And His Word will never fail us. We can stand on it. If we remain steadfast and unmovable in His Word, He will give us everything we need. He said that He would open up the windows of Heaven and pour us out a blessing that we would not have room to contain (see Malachi 3:10).

We can always trust God, and we can always trust His Word. He knows what we're going through, and He has made Himself available as our Resource. There have been times in my life when I didn't have anywhere else to turn but to God, and He didn't fail me.

The Bible is not like other books, so before I read it, I always pray for understanding. Then, as I read pages I have read before, God speaks to me and gives me wonderful revelations. I love that. I love it when He helps me by breaking His Word down so that I can understand it on a practical level and then share it with others.

The Power of the Word

The Word of God is always so refreshing. It gives hope, peace, joy, wisdom, knowledge and understanding.

The Word of God has made me bold for Him. It has lifted my faith and made me stronger. I've always been a very quiet person, but when I'm sharing God's Word, I can speak with boldness, confidence and power. It's because I have a personal relationship with the Author Himself, and I know what He can do. He can make the blind to see and the lame to walk, and He can do anything else but fail. I also know that He would never leave or forsake His children.

You, too, must develop or cultivate your relationship with God through prayer and consistent study of His Word. These are powerful resources, because you can go to Him any time of the day or night. Spend time with Him so that you can then know His voice when He speaks to you.

Four years ago I made a personal commitment to God, to wake up each morning between five and six o'clock to pray, to study His Word and to get to know Him for myself. Because of having done this, I can walk with my head up today, not because I'm the pastor's wife, but because I know who I am in the Lord.

Prepare Yourself in the Word

We must always prepare ourselves in God's Word so that we can then minister to others. God's Word is so very powerful. It will make you cry, dance, forgive in your heart and be humble in your spirit. It will also make you laugh again! I feel God's anointing even as I'm writing this chapter. Thank You, Lord, for Your anointing power!

The Word of God will lift your self-esteem and give you hope for tomorrow and for all the desires, goals and visions that you may have. His Word will build you up and let you know that you're His child. He has promised us:

> *But seek first his kingdom and his righteousness, and all these things will be given to you as well.*
>
> Matthew 6:33

Whatever you want, my God has it. Study His Word and trust Him, and it will be yours.

The Word Will Keep You

The Word of God will keep you from temptation and sin. John the Baptist recognized Jesus as *"the Lamb of God who takes away the sin of the world"*:

> *The next day John saw Jesus coming toward him, and said, "Behold! The Lamb of God who takes away the sin of the world!"*
>
> John 1:29, NKJ

There's safety in God's Word, and when it resides in our hearts, it takes away all of our fears. His Word is so reliable that you can "take it to the bank." Trust God and rely on His Word, and you can get through any situation. His Word is real. It's a light in dark places. Out of your suffering will come great substance when you trust God's Word, for you will see His promises for you come to pass.

If you can lay hold of this simple truth, you can be a great first lady.

☞ Journal for Chapter 11 ☜

SCRIPTURE:

But seek first his kingdom and his righteousness, and all these things will be given to you as well.

Matthew 6:33

WORDS OF INSPIRATION:

We must remember to put God first and seek Him through His Word in the good times as well as bad. If we can keep our focus on God and not on our current situation, He promises us that all things will be added unto us. This doesn't just mean material things; it also includes our heart's desires. But remember to seek the Blesser and not the blessing.

REFLECTIONS:

Chapter Twelve

Making Time for Romance

Do not deprive each other except by mutual consent and for a time, so that you may devote yourselves to prayer. Then come together again so that Satan will not tempt you because of your lack of self-control.   1 Corinthians 7:5

Many modern couples have found that with children, community, church and work, they have very little time left over for each other and have to actually schedule time for romance. And, believe it or not, many busy ministers have the same problem. This is a serious matter, for neglecting the marriage can have disastrous results. Paul admonished the Christians of the early Church not to make this mistake. Instead, we must do all that we can to keep the fires of romance burning.

Keep the Fires Burning

Boring! Mundane! Unexciting! Does this describe the current state of your marriage? If you answered yes, then there are many strategies you can employ as a woman to rekindle that fire.

The first strategy I'd recommend is that you actually start dating your husband. I know that traditionally this is something he should be doing, but maybe if you start the ball rolling, he'll catch on and continue the process. At least one night a week, you and your husband should have a date night. That's your night, so do what you want to do. If nothing else, just take a drive together. Share an ice cream cone.

Whatever you like to do together, plan in advance some time that is just for the two of you alone. If you're not already doing this, suggest it to your husband, and watch him run for the car. I promise you that he'll love the idea.

Your Support Is Inspiring

My second suggestion may surprise some women. Encourage your husband in all that he does. First do it because it's pleasing to God, and also do it as a romantic motivator. Encouragement is wonderfully inspiring and can make your relationship much more romantic.

"How's that?" some might ask. Think about this: when a man feels that his wife "has his back" and supports him mentally, physically and emotionally, he can persevere with more determination and strength. But he will also feel more love and affection toward you. More love means more nights and days together and more thoughts of one another through the day. More affection for him thus translates into more attention for you!

So make your man feel like the man of God he is. The Scriptures teach us:

Wives, submit to your husbands as to the Lord. For the husband is the head of the wife as Christ is the head of the church, his body, of which he is the Savior.
Ephesians 5:22-23

Enjoy your husband for who he is in God. Enjoy him for the man you loved and married. God brought this man into your life for you to love. He's the man you fell in love with, the one with whom you wanted to spend the rest of your life. And you're the woman he can lean on.

Give Him Freedom to Be Himself

Give your husband the freedom to be himself, and don't pressure him to be like anyone else. Applaud him and let him know that he's the only one for you. Create memories together again. Bring candles and gifts to special places. Write him love notes and drop them in the car or send him an e-mail that just says, "I love you." Sign it Mrs. _____ (your last name).

When referring to your partnership, use the terms "we" and "us" instead of always making it "you" or "I." Using these inclusive terms shows him that you know you're one, and that will make any husband smile. Be his best friend, so that when you're alone and cuddling, he can talk to you about everything that may be on his heart.

Be a good listener. Stroke his back, head and ego. Smile at him when he looks at you. He'll soon begin to think, "Wow, what a wonderful woman I have!"

At the very least, kiss him every morning before either of you leave the house and every night before bed. If you happen to be in separate locations at bedtime, call and kiss him goodnight over the phone. That will make him want to hurry home to you. Make him feel and understand that you need and love him forever. Then, when he does come home, he'll come straight to you.

Love notes, phone calls and e-mails are all media through which you can communicate loving thoughts and romantic words. Everyone wants to be loved, and your husband is no different. It is your love that will turn him on.

Be Generous with Your Love

Ask God to motivate you to be generous with your

husband. Realize that if you treat him great, he'll respond in kind to you. Dress attractively just for him. Eat well, take vitamins and get the proper amount of rest, and do it all for him.

Find ways to work through personal stress so that you have energy left over for him. Create and experiment with new ideas for romance so that you never settle into a routine. However, if for some reason the flame dims, acknowledge the problem and then identify strategies to work through it. Pray and ask for direction from God, or take it a step further and seek the advice of godly counselors. Love is great when both partners are trying to make it work, so keep that fire burning.

King Solomon described how each of us should want our love to be:

Place me like a seal over your heart, like a seal on your arm;
for love is as strong as death, its jealousy unyielding as the grave.
It burns like blazing fire, like a mighty flame.

Song of Solomon 8:6

Do whatever is necessary to keep that kind of love burning in your marriage.

If you can lay hold of this simple truth, you can be a great first lady.

Journal for Chapter 12

SCRIPTURE:

Do not deprive each other except by mutual consent and for a time, so that you may devote yourselves to prayer. Then come together again so that Satan will not tempt you because of your lack of self-control.

1 Corinthians 7:5

WORDS OF INSPIRATION:

Keep surprises, spontaneity, excitement and happiness in your marriage. Make sure your spouse knows that you're satisfied with him and that you enjoy your life together.

REFLECTIONS:

Chapter Thirteen

Making Time for the PKs

A good man leaves an inheritance for his children's children.   Proverbs 13:22

The children of pastors are forced to go through many adjustments, just as we are. They didn't ask for their parents to be pastors or for themselves to be thought of as examples, but suddenly there they are living in a fish bowl of sorts. Their parents are so stretched for time by their many responsibilities that they often don't have time for them (their own children)—or so it seems. For this reason pastors' kids (or PKs, as they're often called) face many unique emotional and spiritual struggles, and sometimes it's more than they can handle. If you love your children, you won't let this happen to them.

Expectations

Everyone expects PKs to act a certain way and to be a certain way. They're expected to be good children who make good grades and have good conduct, but inside they're just normal human beings like everyone else, with normal hopes and dreams. They want to live, and sometimes the church responsibilities their parents have undertaken seem to complicate their lives so much that they find their opportunities limited.

As PKs, these children must not only deal with their own particular set of issues. They have to represent their parents and the church. Because of this, all eyes are upon them, and this understandably creates a lot of extra tension in their lives.

PKs Get It from All Sides

Interestingly, church members seem to feel that they have the right to correct the pastor's children at every turn. Some refer to the PKs as "the worst kids in the church, " and everything they do, good or bad, becomes a "big deal." They're crucified for every wrongdoing, and they cannot ever make any mistakes. This seems to go against what Paul taught the early Church:

*Fathers, provoke not your children to anger, lest they
be discouraged.*   Colossians 3:21, KJV

For some reason, members have no reservation about
going to the pastor about his children and their actions.
Sometimes, when members are upset with the pastor and
his wife, they actually take it out on the children. This
makes me want to say to them, "Please leave my kids
alone, and let them be kids."

Our children are accountable to us, their parents, and
they know well what the Bible teaches:

*Honor your father and mother, which is the first com-
mandment with promise.*   Ephesians 6:2, NKJ

Like their mothers, PKs are expected to take leadership roles in the church, whether or not they feel they
have gifts in that particular area. They're often forced to
take church responsibilities on top of all their other responsibilities—in the home, in the school and in the
community. Now, along with their homework and household chores and whatever other outside interests they
may be pursuing, they also have to attend more meetings, complete more assignments and meet more
deadlines. At times I, as a mother, have wondered:

- When do they ever have a break?
- When can they just be children?
- Do they have a voice in anything, or must they just

live with the hand they're dealt?
• Is this all fair to them?

Neglected Children

On top of everything else, PKs see that the pastor, their father, seems to have time for everyone else's children but his own. He does what he can to speak into the lives of the children of his members, pray with them when they have a need and offer them guidance for their daily lives. At the same time, all too often, his own children are receiving only the bare essentials from him.

Some pastors seem to be raising other members' children, even offering to pay for their school fees, books and other needs. But can it be right that his own children are not having their physical, emotional and spiritual needs met? Ministry to others is important, and we must do it, but how can we afford to minister to everyone else and not to our own?

Please don't misunderstand what I'm saying. We, as pastors and first ladies, make many sacrifices for the ministry, and our children will also be expected to make some. We know that the rewards for our sacrifice will be great, and that should be the same for PKs. But neglect is neglect, and neglecting our children can never be pleasing to God. Charity must first begin at home.

Do other people have to mentor your children because you're so busy in the ministry that you don't have time for them? Remember that you are parents first and ministers second. Your first responsibility is to your own.

Give Your Children a Break

Give your children a break, literally and figuratively. Sometimes they just need to get away from church activities and spend some quality time together with you as Mom and Dad or with friends and neighbors. There's more to life than going to church. Sometimes they just need to be free to speak, to laugh and to enjoy life, and not to feel like they're part of some drill team every single moment.

Eventually, your children will grow up and have families of their own, and you don't want them to take any negative attitudes against the church into the next generation. Pray for your children, teach them the Word of God and expect them to follow the Lord, but at the same time, allow them the same opportunities that other children in the neighborhood have.

Our children are our future, and if we faithfully fulfill our duties to them now, they will grow up and take care of us, while teaching our grandchildren the importance of the Christian life and ministry. In this way, our influence will be guaranteed for many generations.

But in the meantime, we must allow our children to find their own identity as it relates to achieving unique goals God may have placed in their hearts. They must make their own decisions in life, and it is those decisions that will ultimately empower them to become mature and useful adults. Giving them this freedom will allow them to have zeal as they pursue and reach their personal destiny.

Train Them Up

The Proverbs leave us a strong charge:

Train up a child in the way he should go, and when he is old he will not depart from it.   Proverbs 22:6, NKJ

Nothing can erase or negate our responsibility to our children. We must serve as examples for them, and that will happen whether we like it or not. What they see their mother and father doing is what they will do. Eating right, exercising, demonstrating good character, loving each other, spending quality time with the family, praying together, studying God's Word together and walking in excellence are some of the values we should be instilling in our children now. They are products of us, so let them see you lead with integrity, and they will become great leaders themselves.

Speak Positively Into Their Lives

Finally, it's so very important that we speak good things

into our children's lives. We should never be guilty of saying things like, "You're so bad that you'll never be able to do that." Instead, we should speak positively. Tell your children, "You're very intelligent," "You're so handsome [or so beautiful]." When they fail, as they surely must at some point, tell them, "It's okay, try again. You'll achieve it." Such validations will speak into their destiny, and don't allow anyone else to speak differently into their lives.

In every congregation, it's important that the children feel a part of things and that they not be overlooked and slighted as insignificant or unimportant. They're our future.

If you can lay hold of this simple truth, you can be a great first lady.

Journal for Chapter 13

SCRIPTURE:

A good man leaves an inheritance for his children's children, but a sinner's wealth is stored up for the righteous.   Proverbs 13:22

WORDS OF INSPIRATION:

Charity begins at home. If we can't show Christ's love to our own children, how can we be effective leaders of the church?

REFLECTIONS:

_____

_____

_____

_____

_____

_____

_____

_____

_____

_____

_____

Chapter Fourteen

Making Time for Household Chores

*So whether you eat or drink or whatever you do, do it
all for the glory of God.*   1 Corinthians 10:31

The Bible has surprisingly little to say about cleanliness, but in every society it has long been regarded that cleanliness is next to godliness in importance. Certainly this is a long-held belief of the American church, so much so that most Christians imagine that this saying is actually part of the Sacred Scriptures. It's not, but it might as well be.

Cleanliness Blesses any Family

Studies have consistently shown that habits of good personal hygiene and good household cleanliness directly affect the health of the entire family. This is one of the continuing struggles in underdeveloped countries, where the lack of good water too often adversely affects not only the health and well-being of newborn babies, but also that of entire populations. We are very blessed in this country to have the means to maintain a good healthy atmosphere in which our families can grow.

First Ladies Are Not Exempt

This means that first ladies, in addition to all of their other responsibilities, have to find time to maintain a clean house. Some first ladies may be able to have their cleaning done for them, and some churches insist on providing this service for their pastors (often through volunteers), but many of us still have household chores.

When we appear at the church for service, we have to be well put together and make sure that our husband and children are also well put together, but in order to accomplish this, a lot of behind-the-scenes activity is necessary. There are a lot of loads of clothes put into and out of the washer and dryer, a lot of clothes are ironed and/or folded and put away, and a lot of trips are made to the cleaners. It's all done to the glory of God.

First Ladies' Families Need to Eat

Pastors and their wives do sometimes fast, but they

are human like everyone else, and they need to eat. This requires meal planning, shopping, cooking and serving, and the more mouths you have to feed the more complicated this process can get.

Feeding a growing family takes a lot of organization, and many of us lack organizational skills. What can we do? Ask God to help you. He will. It's all for His glory, so we want to do it well.

Our Houses Are Reflections of Who We Are

A first lady, as elegant as she may seem in public, must take the time to make sure that her personal environment reflects who she really is, that it is a direct reflection of her elegance. Her household, therefore, should possess and portray qualities of the lady herself. She is not just the humble lady we see in public; she is a lady who knows she has a job to do, and so she sets forth every morning with her required chores in mind and accomplishes them.

Houses that are poorly kept and unclean don't reflect well upon their owner. If a first lady "has it all together" in church, then she must "have it all together" at home as well. Just as you see her, so should her house be.

Again, this all requires organization. The first thing most of us need to do on a daily basis is to prepare a checklist of everything that must be done that particular day. First ladies must be professional about everything they do, and this includes the way we serve our families at home.

Just as in the church, everything in a first lady's house must be done with excellence. She must take the time to make sure that her husband and children have clean garments. She must also make sure that everything smells fresh and clean. Then, by the end of each day, she must prepare an evening meal for her family. When the day is done, a first lady should feel confident that her house is clean and everyone in it is well-fed.

Spiritual Household Chores

As everyone knows, keeping ourselves and our environment clean, neat and organized doesn't only relate to physical housework; this is something that God expects of us spiritually as well. It's not enough to have the house free from clutter and dirt; the environment and atmosphere of the house must also be clean and free of sin. This will affect every member of the family—from the top to the very bottom—for good or for bad.

Every first lady, therefore, must bring all of her proverbial "dirty laundry" to God, and the only way to do that effectively is through prayer. A first lady must ensure that her house is clean by staying before God in intercession for herself and every other member of her household.

"Why does she have to do that?" some might ask.

"Aren't they all protected by God." A pastor's family is just as susceptible to sin as any other family, and, in many cases, the danger may be even more grave. Satan loves nothing more than causing hurt and pain in the home of a leader, the example. In this way, he hopes to harm the entire church.

Although your husband may be a pastor, he is first of all a human being, and human beings are susceptible to sin. We all know that there is an awful lot of temptation in the world around us, and the sad truth is that temptation is also to be found within the walls of the church itself. The church is made up of people, the ministries of the church are to people, and people have problems and are sinful. Every first lady must spend time asking God to keep her man holy. She knows and she trusts him, but she's often the power behind the throne. Where you find a good man, there's usually a good woman behind him to support and undergird him.

Take Special Care with Your Children

As for her children, a first lady must keep them close, as well as being constantly alert to the wiles of the enemy. Without motherly prayers and guidance, as well as the application of the teachings brought forth by their father and pastor, children may well be tempted to stray. They are easily influenced, and a first lady, as their mother, knows this. She must, therefore, spend quality time with God on their behalf, to ensure that her children choose the correct path and that, with the help of the Lord, she and her husband are able to positively influence their life decisions.

So the domestic chores of a first lady are not only manual labor, but spiritual labor as well. Cleanliness is next to godliness in more ways than one!

If you can lay hold of this simple truth, you can be a great first lady.

Journal for Chapter 14

SCRIPTURE:

So whether you eat or drink or whatever you do, do it all for the glory of God. 1 Corinthians 10:31

WORDS OF INSPIRATION:

Always maintain a clean and pure spiritual and physical house, remembering that cleanliness is next to godliness.

REFLECTIONS:

_____

_____

_____

_____

_____

_____

_____

_____

_____

_____

_____

_____

Chapter Fifteen

Making Time for Vacations

The LORD turn his face toward you and give you peace.
Numbers 6:26

Staying on the go with the children, working, paying the bills and maintaining the personal and church families can all be hard work for both the pastor and his wife. We're often so busy that we don't take time out just to relax and unwind. Everyone needs a vacation once in a while. Such a vacation could be time to listen, to love, to snuggle, to play or just to do nothing together.

Plan Time Together

Has it been months or years since your husband has had you to himself for a vacation? If so, surprise him with the idea or with a more precise plan. Note: check his schedule first, so that you're not the one surprised!

Make time for a little vacation, even if it's just to get away for one night. Plan a short (or long) vacation away from the hustle and bustle of life with just you and your husband. Take the time to let him release his mind from his cares and relax. He needs some time alone with you.

As we know, when the foundation of any marriage begins to crumble, everything else will fall too. So plan a getaway, just to talk, laugh and have fun, enjoying each other's company. Learn more about each other, and take time to reconnect emotionally. Share everything that you've been doing without each other lately. Talk endlessly and listen to each other's dreams. Whatever you do doesn't have to be expensive or extravagant.

Be Friends, as Well as Lovers

Marriage is based on friendship, which has the power to endure time. Passion is important, but friendship is a strong sealant. Friends listen to each other, make sacrifices, have no hidden agendas and can always be counted on. And, very importantly, friends overlook the small "stuff" that doesn't matter. So be his friend! Give each other love unconditionally. Share your souls. Show affection and respect for each other. True friendship is the cement that will hold you together through the tests of time.

When life is good, enjoy it. Learn to be content with what you have, and live in the moment. Dreams will still continue, but during your getaway, just focus on you and him, sharing, loving, listening, playing and "grooving" together. Do something he's been wanting to do for a long time, but hasn't had the time or the money to do it. Take him somewhere that you know he can have fun, like the beach or the mountains. Occasionally, break the rule of doing it, just the two of you, and visit with friends he enjoys being around.

Making the Decision

Many ministers have a hard time actually making the decision to take a vacation however long, because of their vision for God's Kingdom and their burden for hurting people everywhere. There are always more lost to win, more sick to be prayed for and more couples with marital problems to be resolved. But we have to think of ourselves too. If we're not our best, how can we minister to others effectively? If we fail, what will happen to them?

Whatever you choose to do, be spontaneous. Be boisterous. Be bold. Make it a fun time for both of you. If relaxation is what you need, try a bed and breakfast or a private room at a hotel for a night or the weekend. Go on an adventure. God doesn't limit your joy, so why should you?

If you can lay hold of this simple truth, you can be a great first lady.

⌒ Journal for Chapter 15 ⌒

SCRIPTURE:

The LORD turn his face toward you and give you peace.

Numbers 6:26

WORDS OF INSPIRATION:

When you go on vacation with your spouse, rest, relax and restore yourselves. Have fun! Do everything or do nothing together. Just share quiet time with each other.

REFLECTIONS:

_____

_____

_____

_____

_____

_____

_____

_____

_____

_____

Chapter Sixteen

Making Time for Yourself

But Jesus often withdrew to lonely places and prayed.
Luke 5:16

Often, for those in ministry, there seems to be time for everyone else and everything else but ourselves. But when do we recharge our own batteries?

Reserving "Me Time"

For as far back as I can remember, I've treasured what I like to call "me time." Every morning, for instance, I take long walks in the park, just so that I can have some of this "me time." It's a time for me to get off of life's treadmill and walk at my own pace. I also sometimes enjoy pampering myself, reading a book, taking a relaxing bath, shopping or spending quiet time alone with God, just the two of us, one on one.

There are so many roles and responsibilities that a first lady is called upon to fill. Not only is she the pastor's wife and a community leader, but she's also a professional businessperson, a mother, a sister, an aunt, a friend and, in some cases, an entrepreneur. It's not that I don't love and appreciate being a first lady. To the contrary, I do. I have simply learned the art and importance of prioritizing some "me time" in the scheme of things. If I want to be even remotely healthy and content, I must reserve time for myself.

Even Jesus did this. Wherever He and His disciples happened to be, He would seek out some *"lonely [or out-of-the-way] places,"* and talk to His Father. If Jesus needed that, how much more do you and I need it?

Getting Clear Direction

"Me time" is a wonderful time for me to get clear direction from God on how to become a Proverbs 31 woman. Nonstop work, without some breaks, causes stress, irritability, agitation and even depression. "Me time" promotes in me a clarity of thought and aids my capacity to be creative and productive. If you stop for a moment and listen carefully, you just might hear the Lord telling you to relax.

Jesus encouraged His disciples to *"come aside"* (NKJ):

Come with me by yourselves to a quiet place and get some rest.   Mark 6:31

If you don't think you need that, then you know more than Jesus.

"Me time" gives me a positive outlook on life in general. It helps me to appreciate the little things. Today's society has made everything very fast-paced, but in order to be effective, you must have a more balanced outlook. When using the theory of God first, family second, career third, undergirded by sufficient "me time," you are guaranteed to have a well-balanced life.

How to Create "Me Time"

You might be wondering, "How do I create this 'me time'?" You create "me time" by conscientiously putting it into your schedule, making it a priority. There is no other way. Just waiting for it to happen will never produce any results. Make an appointment with yourself in your schedule, and then don't allow other obligations to override that appointment.

Your "me time" is unique to you, so there's no set format that you must use. Start with a small amount of time (say fifteen minutes), and then increase it as you feel comfortable with it. Remember, "me time" is all about you and what makes you feel good. It gives you the opportunity to be in complete control of the moment, setting your own pace and agenda.

After taking some "me time," I feel refreshed, renewed, relaxed, energized, focused and, most importantly, spiritually connected. It lets me know and appreciate who I am as a person. It points me in the direction of my true purpose and destiny. When my "me time" is over, I'm ready to continue with the plans God has set before me. And I want to be ready for whatever He wants me to do!

If you can lay hold of this simple truth, you can be a great first lady.

⟜ Journal for Chapter 16 ⟞

SCRIPTURE:

Then, because so many people were coming and going that they did not even have a chance to eat, he said to them, "Come with me by yourselves to a quiet place and get some rest." Mark 6:31

WORDS OF INSPIRATION:

Jesus saw the need for time alone, and He also called His disciples aside for times of relaxation and reflection. If you are not fresh and renewed yourself, how can you help others with their problems?

REFLECTIONS:

_____

_____

_____

_____

_____

_____

_____

_____

Chapter Seventeen

Making Time for Health

Beloved, I wish above all things that thou mayest prosper and be in health, even as thy soul prospereth.

3 John 1:2, KJV

It's surprising how many ministers and minister's wives get so busy doing the Lord's work that they seemingly can't find time to maintain their own health. This is very foolish because, if our health fails, how can we do the work the Lord has entrusted to us?

A Responsibility We Must Never Neglect

Taking care of ourselves is a responsibility that we must never neglect. For one thing, we must choose to implement exercise habits that lead to vigor and health. Research indicates that by making the right choices now, we can add healthy, active and vibrant years to our lives. These appropriate health choices will not only make us feel better, but also look better. We cannot give this subject the space it deserves in a book like this, but let us, at least, take a look at some general ground rules that could increase and help maintain good overall health for our whole family.

Changing Some Old Habits

Committing to a healthier life-style requires that we change several of our old habits, especially those related to our eating. A good way to start changing those habits would be to keep a journal for a week, jotting down details about what, when, where, why and how you eat. Ask yourself questions like these:

- Did I eat just because I was depressed?
- Did I eat out of boredom?
- Do others tempt me with food or force foods on me that I know are not healthy?
- What types of food do I sometimes overeat?
- Which beneficial foods am I neglecting?

The result of an honest self-evaluation like this one can then guide us in conscious decisions for change. If we can take time to study our former and current eating habits, we can then see where we're going wrong and attempt to alter our eating habits in the days to come.

It often helps to discuss such a life-altering decision with members of the family, first in order to rally their support and encouragement, and second, to see if such a change might benefit them as well.

Common Recommendations

One of the most common recommendations of nutritionists is that we all eat a healthy breakfast each morning. Studies have consistently shown that people who don't eat breakfast have metabolic rates four to five percent below normal, and that can translate into weight gain, high blood pressure and even heart problems down the road. Just think, not taking time for breakfast could be adding eight or more pounds to your overall weight each year.

Here are some other ideas that most experts agree on that can positively alter your daily diet for improved overall health:

- Decrease your intake of carbohydrates (rice, potatoes and pasta).
- Reduce your intake of sweets.
- Limit your bread and soda consumption.
- Drink plenty of water (half of your body weight in ounces is considered optimal).

- Eliminate fried foods from your diet as much as possible.
- Increase chicken and fish intake and reduce red meat intake.
- Eat egg whites without the yolk, to reduce the intake of cholesterol.

Maintaining a daily regimen similar to this has been proven to increase the longevity and efficacy of your mental, physical and spiritual life.

Exercise! Just Do It!

Next, many studies show that people who exercise regularly live longer. There is no strong consensus on just how much exercise you need or the intensity of the exercise required, but accept the fact that you must get some physical exercise. That's all there is to it. You must do it. You must! You must!

Exercise strengthens your heart, boosts your immune system and helps prevent many age-related illnesses. You, your spouse and your whole family should implement a regular exercise regimen. This will help you to:

- Improve your overall health
- Slow the aging process
- Boost weight loss
- Enhance stamina

- Effectively cope with stress
- Heighten mental clarity
- Promote happy feelings
- Improve work efficiency
- Improve memory
- Increase sexual pleasure
- Eliminate fatigue
- Increase energy
- Dramatically improve the overall quality of life

Good health habits are especially important for a pastor and his wife because the two of them serve as role models for the entire church. Also, God needs them to be emotionally, physically, mentally and spiritually alert and on guard so that they can do His work.

A Well-Being Self-Examination

To see how you're doing, try giving yourself a little well-being self-examination:

1. Is what I'm eating pleasing to God?
2. Will my diet nourish my body so that I can be efficient in His service?
3. Will my life-style make my mind keener, my muscles stronger, my judgment more sound and my influence for the Lord more potent?

Not only should our spiritual temples be clean, but our physical ones as well, so that we might serve the Lord without any hindrances. When eating right and exercising regularly, you will be alert, focused and available to recognize the tricks and schemes of the enemy. Every pastor and first lady must stay sharp and prepared so that when they are called upon to serve, they will be ready. Isaiah wrote:

> *Lord, your discipline is good, for it leads to life and health. You have restored my health and have allowed me to live!*   Isaiah 38:16, NLT

When we take the required time and make the required effort to maintain a healthy life-style, it lets the Lord know how much we appreciate Him giving us this wonderful life, and that we intend to make the best of it for His glory.

Special Problems

Pastors and first ladies are often called upon to fellowship with others through dining out. Their schedule is extremely busy, so they may not be as physically active as is ideal for good health. If they continue to eat out frequently and fail to get the proper exercise, weight gain is inevitable. There are little things we can do to help ourselves. Choose to walk short distances rather than ride. Take the stairs instead of the elevator. If you can find some exercise routine that suits you, make a commitment to it and stick to that commitment. Choosing to exercise together as husband and wife is an excellent way to share and fellowship with one another without outside distractions.

Learn how to relax and rest. Enjoy one another. Make a conscientious effort to take your minds off of your work and focus your attention on each other. This will release stress and contribute to healthy living, so you can be fresh for God.

Get Regular Checkups

Scheduling regular visits with your doctor and your dentist is a vital part of maintaining good health. Doctors can give you the resources to help you monitor your health at home. This can help avoid preventable medical conditions.

Should you already have a medical condition, your doctor can help you develop a plan that will keep you as healthy as possible with that condition. Visit your dentist regularly for routine cleaning and dental hygiene maintenance. It's not only important to your appearance, but also to your overall health.

Maintain a Healthy Attitude

Finally, the most important ingredient to having and maintaining good health is your attitude. Your commitment to better health must be coupled with a positive attitude. This will boost your discipline for implementing the right diet and exercise for you.

If you can lay hold of this simple truth, you can be a great first lady.

Journal for Chapter 17

SCRIPTURE:

Beloved, I wish above all things that thou mayest prosper and be in health, even as thy soul prospereth.

3 John 1:2, KJV

WORDS OF INSPIRATION:

Even as we continue to grow in God spiritually, we must develop and maintain good eating habits and an exercise regimen that will keep us in good health.

REFLECTIONS:

_____

_____

_____

_____

_____

_____

_____

_____

_____

_____

_____

Chapter Eighteen

Making Time for Healing

Now unto him that is able to do exceeding abundantly above all that we ask or think, according to the power that worketh in us, Unto him be glory in the church by Christ Jesus throughout all ages, world without end. Amen.

Ephesians 3:20-21, KJV

As much as we might strive to protect our health, first ladies and their families get sick, like anyone else. In the moment that any sickness comes to us, there are at least two very good reasons to believe God for our healing: (1) We have a great work to do, so we cannot afford to lose our health or, worse, lose our life. (2) Healing is for every believer, and when we in the ministry demonstrate God's goodness in this regard, it inspires others to be healed from their sicknesses as well.

It's My Prerogative!

A Bad Report

When a doctor gives us his bad report, immediately our flesh reacts, and we begin to hold our face in fear and tremble. Our minds think, "What do I do now? What about my husband, my children, my family and my friends?" But in such moments, we must stop and think about the goodness of God and all that He can do. He can do everything but fail.

The apostle Paul reminded us that God *"is able to do exceeding abundantly above all that we ask or think."* Wow! That's why we can declare, *"by His stripes we are healed"* (see Isaiah 53:5 and 1 Peter 2:24). We can ask for anything, and our God will answer us, and He's always on time. If we can keep our mind stayed on Him and praise Him in spite of our circumstances, we will receive deliverance and prosperity. But what steps can we take to achieve healing? Here are three positive steps to take:

Maintain a Healthy Attitude

A healthy mind is good for the body and soul. Encourage yourself with God's promises:

O LORD my God, I cried unto thee, and thou hast healed me.
O LORD, thou hast brought up my soul from the grave:

thou hast kept me alive, that I should not go down to the pit.

Sing unto the LORD, *O ye saints of his, and give thanks at the remembrance of his holiness.*

For his anger endureth but a moment; in his favour is life: weeping may endure for a night, but joy cometh in the morning.   Psalms 30:2-5, KJV

You can affirm yourself daily, speaking your deliverance into existence by saying, "I am healed, happy and whole. I am walking in my healthy and wealthy place. My soul is saying hallelujah that my body is free from cancer and disease." The decision is yours. Whose report will you believe? Choose to believe the report of the Lord.

Let Faith Arise in Your Heart

Let your faith rise. The Scriptures teach us:

Now faith is the substance of things hoped for, the evidence of things not seen.   Hebrews 11:1, KJV

We must speak that we are healed, set free and walking in complete and total victory. We must make up our minds and assure our spirits that God is in control. Our thoughts and words have the power to dictate to our environments. Therefore, affirming our faith daily will filter our thoughts to reflect the knowledge and understanding of the abundance of God for our lives. Then, our words can take over.

Declare It

Always remember just how powerful the tongue is:

The tongue has the power of life and death, and those who love it will eat its fruit.   Proverbs 18:21

So first get it into your spirit, let it build your faith and then declare it to be so. This does not mean that your faith will not be tested. It surely will be.

My Own Test

My own test came very unexpectedly. My doctor called one day to say, "I'd like for you to come back to the clinic. We saw something on your mammogram that doesn't look good, and we need to discuss it. In fact, I'd like to repeat the mammogram if you don't mind."

I'll have to admit that when I heard those words, I was frightened. I began to pray and plead the blood of Jesus over my body. I worried, but I also cried out to God for my healing. As I did so, I felt a release in my spirit, letting me know that everything was going to be all right. My faith was strong, and my mind said, "You are healed."

I went back to the doctor to receive another mammogram, and the results revealed that I had what she called a lymphoid but that it was benign. This meant that there was no cancer. I began to praise God right there in the doctor's office, and she just looked at me and smiled.

As a leading lady, we must make every effort to keep our faith intact at all times. You never know when the enemy will try to attack your family. If the God we serve could make the lame walk and the blind see and heal a woman with an issue of blood, He can heal us too. So whose report will we believe? We will believe the report of the Lord.

How do we receive our healing and the manifestation of God's Word in our lives? We receive healing through praying, visualizing it in our minds, speaking it with our mouths and then waiting patiently on the materialization. Say to yourself, "My soul says, 'Yes, Lord.' I have the victory." Praise God in advance.

God's Word promises:

> *He who has an ear, let him hear what the Spirit says to the churches. To him who overcomes, I will give the right to eat from the tree of life, which is in the paradise of God.*   Revelation 2:7

Now my sleep is sweet because I've received my healing. Don't ever lose your praise. While enduring your pain, you can experience deliverance, peace, healing and joy. Praise God while you're still in your battle, for the battle is not yours, but the Lord's. God always has the last word, so there's power in prayer.

My Sister's Trial

In April of 2007, my sister, Lady Tawana Rose, was diagnosed with cancer. The doctors gave her only about six months to live. Of course, we refused to receive that report, for the devil is a liar. Backed up by the prayers of her family and friends, she demonstrated extraordinary faith and refused to give up. Instead, she remained strong, standing on the Word of God for her healing.

Lady Tawana went through chemotherapy treatments, but as a result of the prayers and support offered to her by others and her extraordinary faith, doctors were amazed at her high blood count. Not long before this book went to press, medical personnel called to give her some very good news: There was no more cancer in her body. By His stripes we are healed! So, whose report will you believe?

During the period when Tawana was going through the chemotherapy treatments, she saw many others who were experiencing the same thing, but their faith was not nearly as strong as hers. She had the opportunity to minister to some of them and encourage them. She looked at me one day and said, "I know now why I'm going through this. God has me on an assignment, and I'm honored that He chose me."

When she said that, chills ran through my body, and I said to myself, "What extraordinary faith!" And because of her faith, my sister walks in total healing today. She is a survivor, a strong woman with a mighty testimony for God. She represents His amazing grace.

She is a giver, she loves people, she's an awesome prayer warrior and an awesome mother and wife, and I am encouraged by her faith.

Healing Inspiration Points for the Mind, Body and Soul

Here are some healing inspiration points that will serve us all well, remembering the scripture truth:

So then faith cometh by hearing, and hearing by the word of God.   Romans 10:17, KJV

These strategies can strengthen your personal walk with God. I have used several of these for my own personal growth and development:

- Listen to praise and worship CDs.
- Listen to CDs of the healing scriptures.
- Incorporate intercessory prayer as a part of your daily life-style.
- Fast and pray.
- Sing praises to God every day.
- Drink healing water as a point of contact.

- Eat plenty of fruits and vegetables.
- Drink hot water with lemon.
- Always bless your food before you eat.
- Form a special team to pray for your healing every day.
- Read good books like *Prayers That Avail Much* by Germaine Copeland (Tulsa, Oklahoma, Harrison House: 1997)
- Surround yourself with positive people, most of all with family and friends who will give you love and support and help you to believe God for your healing.
- Believe it and receive it. It's yours for the asking!
- Speak it, for *"death and life are in the power of the tongue"* (Proverbs 18:21, KJV).
- Choose to believe the report of the Lord.
- Know that God has the final word.
- Know that your faith and your words are powerful, so use them.

A Prayer Prescription

- Read out loud and praise God.
- Some helpful scriptures to read (Mark 11:24-25, 1 John 5:14-15, Matthew 21:22, Hebrews 4:14-16 and 2 Corinthians 5:7)
- Repeat these every morning and again before bedtime every evening.
- Declare that you are healed!

If God has called you to this work, then He knows that you need your health to accomplish it.

If you can lay hold of this simple truth, you can be a great first lady.

☞ Journal for Chapter 18 ☜

SCRIPTURE:

Now unto him that is able to do exceeding abundantly above all that we ask or think, according to the power that worketh in us.   Ephesians 3:20, KJV

WORDS OF INSPIRATION:

Rejoice in knowing that we can ask God for whatever it is that we need in our daily lives—no matter how small or how large it might be. This includes our healing even from serious or seemingly incurable ailments. We must ask with faith and then persevere in faith, but know that His promise is that we are healed by His stripes.

REFLECTIONS:

_____

_____

_____

_____

_____

_____

_____

_____

Chapter Nineteen

Tools for Making Time

Find some capable, honest men who fear God and hate bribes. Appoint them as judges over groups of one thousand, one hundred, fifty, and ten. These men can serve the people, resolving all the ordinary cases. Anything that is too important or too complicated can be brought to you. But they can take care of the smaller matters themselves.   Exodus 18:21-22, NLT

In order for a husband and wife who are both in ministry to find some balance in their daily lives, they must understand their obligations and prioritize them. Only through some system of prioritization can they ever hope to achieve efficacy in every area of responsibility. Then, once they have established priorities (and prayer is a most important element in the priority setting process), they must then employ any available tools that can help them make time for what's important—for them as a couple, as a family and also as a congregation.

Learn to Delegate

Delegation of responsibilities to others can sometimes help to meet the needs of the church. The pastor and his wife don't have to do everything, and in fact, they can't do everything. Many hands are needed in a large congregation. *"Honest men [and women] who fear God"* can help you carry the load of ministry, making the seemingly-impossible task of serving as pastor and first lady of a growing church much easier.

Choosing the right people is obviously the key to delegation, and God can guide you in this. With such men and women in place, you will quickly find that your daily pressures become much more manageable.

Combining Activities

Are you needed at the church every day? That type of demand can put a terrible strain on family and home life, especially if you're also working to earn money for the family needs. One idea that might bring you some relief is to combine as many weekday ministries as possible into one particular day. That simple act can free up some time on another day for you as a couple or as a family.

Usually our emphasis is on activities, but we should

also have time with no activities. It should be a consistent, disciplined habit for both pastor and wife to take one day off each week and to take a family vacation away from the church at least once a year. (For more ideas on vacations, see Chapter 15, Making Time for Vacations.)

Be Consistent with Your Communications

Consistent and effective communication is also a very essential key to relieving the stress that comes along with being in ministry. As pastor and wife, home and ministry are innately united, so the two of you must view yourselves as a team. This lessens the stress of ministry. Here's a passage that describes the stark differences between the married and the unmarried when it comes to ministry:

> *I would like you to be free from concern. An unmarried man is concerned about the Lord's affairs—how he can please the Lord. But a married man is concerned about the affairs of this world—how he can please his wife—and his interests are divided. An unmarried woman or virgin is concerned about the Lord's affairs: her aim is to be devoted to the Lord in both body and spirit. But a married woman is concerned about the affairs of this world—how she can please her husband.* 1 Corinthians 7:32-34

The fact that you're married can seriously complicate your life. Instead, turn your marriage into a benefit for the church. For example, pastor and wife can strengthen one another when either the one or the other is weak. The best thing they can do for the church is to be strong believers themselves and to build a good home and raise fine children who are an asset to God and to the church. Unless the marriage and the family are given top priority, along with our personal relationship with God, they may get unintentionally moved further and further down the list of priorities. This must not be allowed to happen.

Subbing for Your Hubby

There are times when the pastor will be absent, and on these occasions, his wife can minister in proxy for him. This is an excellent example of teamwork. The first lady, as we shall see in the very next chapter, is her husband's rib. She is an integral part of him. Therefore, there should never be competition or intimidation between the two.

When others see division between pastor and wife, it weakens the ministry as a whole. Work together with your husband to build the Kingdom of God. Where there is unity there is strength. Always remember that you are a team, and then work in that way.

If you can lay hold of this simple truth, you can be a great first lady.

Journal for Chapter 19

SCRIPTURE:

Find some capable, honest men who fear God and hate bribes.
Exodus 18:21, NLT

WORDS OF INSPIRATION:

Learn to prioritize things in their order of importance and then to utilize any tool available to you to lessen the pressure of too many responsibilities. In this way, much more will be accomplished.

REFLECTIONS:

_____

_____

_____

_____

_____

_____

_____

_____

_____

_____

Part IV

*What Does It Mean
to Stand by My Man?*

Chapter Twenty

Learning to Guard His Back

The LORD God said, "It is not good for the man to be alone. I will make a helper suitable for him."
So the LORD God caused the man to fall into a deep sleep; and while he was sleeping, he took one of the man's ribs and closed up the place with flesh. Then the LORD God made a woman from the rib he had taken out of the man, and he brought her to the man.

Genesis 2:18 and 21-22

And Adam said:

"This is now bone of my bones
And flesh of my flesh;
She shall be called Woman,
Because she was taken out of Man."

Genesis 2:23, NKJ

The Greek word *paraklete* refers to one who stands alongside, more precisely, "one who consoles—a comforter" or "one who intercedes on our behalf—an advocate." This word is used in the New Testament and in Christian theology to refer to the presence of the Holy Spirit with us. But in the very same way that the Holy Spirit stands by each of us, we women need to stand by our man. After all, he is flesh of our flesh and bone of our bone. He needs us to be his comforter and his advocate.

We Are His Rib

We know that we were created from the rib of our husbands, therefore we should stand beside him—not in front of him or behind him. This symbolism should mirror what we do in ministry—as well as in our marriages. Nothing should be allowed to come between you and your husband. We were ordained before time to be his helpmeet, through good times and bad times, through all ups and downs.

We are our husband's number one armor bearer. We should be his eyes and ears at all times, especially while he is preaching and ministering to God's people. As we see people's lives transformed, healings manifested, marriages restored and families reunited, we should be interceding, praying and watching out for him. God has placed an awesome task upon him and is holding him responsible for the people to whom he ministers. We're there to help him.

We, as wives and helpmeets, cannot depend on anyone else to pick up the slack for us. We should always pray for our husbands and be right there for them, watching and standing guard. God will honor our obedience, and so will our husbands.

Baby, "I've Got Your Back."

If a pastor's not doing what he's called to do for his wife, his family, his church or the Body of Christ as a whole, God will deal with him. We must still do our part. Let your husband know, "Baby, 'I've got your back.' " It doesn't matter who else is around him, intending to cover him. They can't compare to your being there for him. Once we know that he's okay, we can then go on and tend to our other responsibilities. Our intent is never to smother him. When you take care of the home and be the wife and mother that God has ordained you to be, He will take care of you and everything that concerns you.

Support the Vision

My husband knows that I believe in what God has given him to do for the Kingdom. He's a visionary, and I support him and the vision God has placed in him wholeheartedly. Without a vision, the people will perish (see Proverbs 29:18), and it is my husband's responsibility to carry that vision to fruition. I'm there to support his vision and his efforts to carry out that vision.

It's never wise to compare our churches with other churches or to compare our husband with other pastors. We have to follow what God has mandated for us, not for others. So build him up at all times, and encourage him in every facet of the ministry. Simply letting him know that you "have his back" will go a long way to make his day.

If you can lay hold of this simple truth, you can be a great first lady.

Journal for Chapter 20

SCRIPTURE:

The man said,

*"This is now bone of my bones
and flesh of my flesh;
she shall be called 'woman,'
for she was taken out of man."*

Genesis 2:23

WORDS OF INSPIRATION:

We are our husband's number one armor bearer, so we must never cease to watch and pray for him.

REFLECTIONS:

_____

_____

_____

_____

_____

_____

_____

_____

_____

Chapter Twenty-One

Learning to Trust Him

Only in his hometown and in his own house is a prophet without honor.   Matthew 13:57

If there is no trust between husband and wife, both of you will be hindered in what you need to be doing for God's Kingdom. Something must be done to regain any trust that has been lost and then to maintain that trust.

For her part, the first lady must be sure that she has her priorities straight. She must trust God to reveal to her any area that could endanger the marriage. And then she must focus on her area of responsibility, whatever God has assigned her to do. Her ministry cannot grow if she is constantly chasing after her husband, wondering what he "might" be doing. You have to learn to trust him, but, more importantly, you have to learn to trust the God in him! Men fail, but God never does.

Our Husbands Will Minister to Other Women

When there is infidelity or some other trust-destroy-
ing occurrence in a marriage, the decision to stick it out
and believe for a better tomorrow is a difficult and delicate one for any woman—even one who is saved. When
we're in the ministry, there is a higher consideration: our
husbands are called by God. This gives us a special reason to act with caution. There is more at stake than our
personal dignity.

But the fact that our husbands are in ministry also
presents a dilemma. Women make up more than half of
the population of the world, and women attend church
more often than men, so our husbands will, without a
doubt, be required to minister to other women. If we
allow a spirit of insecurity and jealousy to creep into our
thinking, even if we have no reason to suspect that he is
doing anything other than what God has instructed him
to do, it can only mean problems for the marriage and for
the ministry. Whenever those spirits try to torment you
and those thoughts try to creep into your mind, immediately ask God to cover your mind with His blood and to
renew a right spirit within you (see Psalm 51:10).

A Type of Spiritual Warfare

What you are experiencing is a type of spiritual warfare. The enemy will use any strategy he can to distract

both you and your husband from walking in your callings, and it is your job to keep yourself and your husband covered with the blood of Jesus every single day. Because you cannot be with him twenty-four hours a day, you have to learn to trust him—when he is with you and when he is away from you.

To do this, you must first know who you are in God and know that your marriage is a healthy one. If you are on top of your responsibilities as a wife, then your husband shouldn't have any reason to do anything outside of the will of God. Just keep walking in truth, and remind yourself of what a precious jewel you are.

That doesn't mean that we should just sit back and do nothing. We must continue in prayer, because the enemy is always busy. He wants us to be unforgiving, accusatory and demanding, for his ultimate goal is to destroy our marriages through divorce. Our tenacity and resilience to stay in the marriage angers the enemy, and he will do anything to get into our mind and thoughts to trick us.

Restoring a Damaged Marriage

When the marriage has been damaged, you and your husband must both make a commitment to work on it, and you must be honest with one another in the process. You may also need to resort to spiritual, or even professional, counseling. Do whatever it takes. Mending what has damaged your relationship will not be easy, and there may be plenty of ups and downs as you work at it, but the marriage can be restored and strengthened through prayer, love, mutual support, communication and understanding.

Later, don't risk distancing your husband by constantly bringing up his faults and failures. Allow him room to be forgiven and restored, just as our heavenly Father does with each of us (you included). Recommit to each other constantly, and make the promise to yourself daily to work on your marriage. Then do it.

If you really want to save your marriage, you can, and if you really want to learn to trust your husband again, you can. If God called him by name and entrusted to him this great ministry, then who are you not to give him the benefit of the doubt?

Keeping Your Husband's Attention

There is a combination of things that we, as wives, must commit to doing to keep our husband's attention. Even though our lives are all about ministry, we still have a responsibility to minister to his total needs. We must make it a habit to build him up and help him realize how special he truly is. This will guarantee that you are on his mind.

If you can lay hold of this simple truth, you can be a great first lady.

Journal for Chapter 21

SCRIPTURE:

Only in his hometown and in his own house is a prophet without honor.   Matthew 13:57

WORDS OF INSPIRATION:

When we apply unconditional love and trust to our marriages, our spouse will know that we have given him and the marriage a new lease on life. Give hope, love, and trust to your husband, and watch God work it all out for you.

REFLECTIONS:

_____

_____

_____

_____

_____

_____

_____

_____

_____

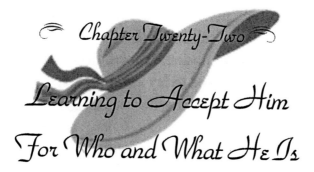

Chapter Twenty-Two

Learning to Accept Him For Who and What He Is

Submit to one another out of reverence for Christ.
Ephesians 5:21

The role of first lady definitely has its challenges, and one of them is how you view your husband. In the public, he is seen as a great leader and an awesome man of God, but in private it may be a very different story. You know him better than anyone else, and this means that you know all his weaknesses, as well as his strengths. Because of this, you may feel like he's a hypocrite and that you're a hypocrite for supporting him. What should your attitude be?

Submit to One Another

The Scriptures call on us to *"submit to one another."*

You, as his wife, are to submit to him (even though he is a frail human being), but he, as your husband, is to submit to you (even though you are also a frail human being). Your level of submission may be somewhat greater than his, and there's a reason for that.

In everything there must be a head, only one, and God has chosen man for that role. Therefore, He has instructed wives to submit to their husband's leadership. This does not leave husbands totally off the hook. They are commanded by God to lay aside their own interests to care for the needs of their wife and family. This is a great sacrifice too.

But what happens when you're sitting in church listening to your husband preach a sermon or teach a class, and the two of you were just engaged in an argument on your way to church or in his office before he entered the pulpit? Do you listen with an attitude of contempt, or do you pray for him as he preaches and teaches? Can you and will you be there to support your man when he needs you the most? It's a difficult question. If you have a difficult marriage, then prayer is the only answer.

Paul taught the early Church:

> *We are not fighting against people made of flesh and blood, but against the evil rulers and authorities of the unseen world, against those mighty powers of darkness who rule this world, and against wicked spirits in the heavenly realms.* Ephesians 6:12, NLT

Your fight is not against your husband, and his fight is not against you. We're all in a heavenly battle with eternal stakes. Therefore, you have a responsibility to walk upright before God so that your prayers can be heard and answered. Make sure that you don't have some skeletons hiding in your own closet before you start trying to deal with the skeletons in someone else's closet.

Examine Yourself Daily

As first ladies, we must examine ourselves daily if we want our prayers, as God's righteous, to avail much. If we are consistently praying and believing for our husband to change, and those prayers don't seem to be manifesting, we may want to take a good look at the woman in the mirror. If your own life lines up with God's Word, as a child of God, wife, woman and mother, then He's obligated to answer your prayers.

God has chosen us to be our husband's number one intercessor. So through prayer and strength from God, we must live for the substance of things we are hoping for, not for what we currently see.

God didn't make a mistake when He called your husband into ministry. He saw something good in that man's heart, and we must ask Him to show us the same thing. Paul wrote:

*I do not understand what I do. For what I want to do I
do not do, but what I hate I do.*   Romans 7:15

So, even the great apostle Paul was just a man.

When you truly love your husband with all your heart,
soul and spirit, you can't give up on him—especially when
you know what God is doing in him and where God is
taking him (even if he can't see it yet). Eventually you
will reap the benefits of remaining steadfast and
longsuffering. If your husband seems to be preaching one
thing and living something else, give God time to fix him
through your prayers. In the meantime, don't talk about
him or degrade him. Rather, take him to the throne of
God and trust His Word to do its work.

Believe that what God has shown you concerning your
husband will come to fruition. Know that, even through
the difficult times, your prayers are being heard and answered. Believe in God's Word, and watch your prayers
manifest in your husband.

Always keep in mind that this is the man whom God
has assigned to you and designed especially for you to
love, honor and respect. Let him know that you are in his
corner forever. Through prayer, you will align your life
in harmony with God's Word, and you will both reap the
rewards.

If you can lay hold of this simple truth, you can be a
great first lady.

Journal for Chapter 22

SCRIPTURE:

I do not understand what I do. For what I want to do I do not do, but what I hate I do. Romans 7:15

WORDS OF INSPIRATION:

God gives us strength in the areas where we are weak, as we approach Him with a sincere and willing heart. Therefore, we must be patient with the weaknesses of others and give them time to change.

REFLECTIONS:

_____

_____

_____

_____

_____

_____

_____

_____

_____

_____

Chapter Twenty-Three

Learning to Show Him Due Respect

Give to everyone what you owe them ... , and give respect and honor to all to whom it is due.

Romans 13:7, NLT

The wife must respect her husband.

Ephesians 5:33

Everyone wants to be respected, and God commands us to respect those to whom respect is due. First, of course, we must respect Him. Then we must respect our parents. We must respect our elders. We must respect our leaders. This includes government leaders, educational leaders and community leaders, as well as religious leaders. And notice that wives are specifically commanded to respect their husbands. That's where we come in, first ladies.

Respect Due on Two Accounts

Your husband merits your respect on two accounts. First, he merits your respect because he's your husband. And secondly, he merits your respect because he's your pastor. So there's no excuse for you to show him disrespect.

This duty of respect ordained by God is not based on the goodness or rightness of the parents, the government leaders or the particular husband involved. Rather, it is based on the authority God has placed in the hands of these individuals. God has chosen your husband to be your husband, so you need to respect him. It's as simple as that. God has chosen your husband to be your pastor, so you need to respect him. It's due him—whatever you happen to be feeling at the moment.

Wait Until You Get Home

Husbands and wives have issues to discuss, and they have legitimate differences of opinion on a whole variety of subjects. But one of the ways we can show respect to our husbands is to restrict any such discussion to a private setting. We must avoid embarrassing him in public by bringing up painful or potentially explosive issues within the hearing of others. Just wait until you get home to discuss it. That's all. It's the respectful thing to do.

A first lady is a lady first, and so she never airs her dirty laundry in public. Instead, she must remain calm, cool and collected at all times, keeping her emotions under control, when eyes are upon her. She must never let anybody see her sweating under pressure.

Sometimes this can be very difficult, especially if some incident has occurred in the public eye. The easiest thing in the world to do is to lash out with our words, but when we do that, we cause irreparable harm to the image of pastor and first lady, and that means we have damaged God's Kingdom. This is serious business. God demands respect where respect is due, and we must learn to give it.

I would like to explore the elements of respect through an acrostic:

Resolution
Example
Stamina
Prayer
Excellence
Control
Timing

The Letter R

The letter r in *respect* represents *resolution,* which is

defined as "the process of resolving." God wants us to resolve our issues, but He also wants us to resolve them in a way that pleases Him. That would mean that we should do it openly, honestly and without quarreling. So take your problems home and solve them there together.

A first lady never lets on to others about what might be going on between her and her husband. She can't because she has to be an example to all. She must learn how to pray and ask God to give her insight, instead of reacting negatively. In this way, she demonstrates the qualities of the woman of virtue:

Her husband is respected at the city gate, where he takes his seat among the elders of the land.

Proverbs 31:23

The Letter E

The letter e in *respect* represents *example*, defined as "one that serves as a pattern to be imitated." That says it all. A first lady is an example to all the women of the congregation. She upholds the true essence of this definition. When conflict is in the midst, she maintains her composure. She will never allow you to see what is going on between her and her husband, for she is truly a virtuous woman.

The Letter S

The letter s in *respect* represents *stamina*, defined as "staying power and endurance." The stamina of a first lady is great because she knows that she's being watched. Her passion for people is so great that she can withstand whatever obstacles get in her way. She has goals for ministry: (1) To walk hand in hand with God, (2) To walk beside her husband, and (3) To save God's people. Keeping those goals uppermost in her mind allows her to push aside personal frustration and wait until she has opportunity to deal wisely with whatever issues she may have.

The Letter P

The letter p in *respect* represents *prayer*, which means "to address God with adoration, confession, supplication or thanksgiving." A first lady must know how to pray for her husband and for herself, especially if problems arise when they're together out in the public eye. Since they're role models and must be an example to everyone in the congregation, prayer is the best she can do at the moment. And prayer is the way she will prepare herself for the ultimate resolution of the issue.

It can be very difficult to pray for someone when you're angry, but a first lady knows that she has to put everything on the altar and still allow God to use her to the utmost—regardless of the current circumstances. Just by praying for her husband, she is ministering, not only to him, but also to herself. God always answers the prayers of the righteous, so she won't be disappointed.

The Letter E

The letter e in *respect* represents *excellence*, defined as "an excellent or valuable quality virtue." As a first lady, you must walk in excellence, for you are representing the man of God and God Himself. You must uphold your husband's reputation by respecting him, not only as your pastor, but also as your husband and a chosen vessel whom God is using. It's possible to support your husband and still have a fruitful life of your own. By supporting him, you're not losing anything.

The Letter C

The letter c in *respect* means *control*, "to restrain." As we have noted, a first lady is always being watched, and because the watchful eye of the public is always there, a first lady must be careful to remain in control of her emotions at all times. The women of the church are always comparing themselves with her. They watch and mimic her every move, so she must always maintain her composure as she represents God and His man.

The Letter T

Lastly, the letter t in *respect* represents *timing*, which is defined as "selection or the ability to select for maximum effect the precise moment for beginning or doing something." Timing is everything. There's a time and place for everything, and a first lady knows that the public is not a place for a dispute between her and her husband. A first lady knows her place, and she keeps her boundaries intact until she gets home. That is the appropriate time and the appropriate place to discuss whatever it is that has come between the two.

Knowing What to Say and How to Say It

Because she is a virtuous woman, a first lady will know just what to say and just how to say it to begin resolving the issue. For starters, she will speak to her husband with poise and grace, not disparagingly or disrespectfully. In doing this, a woman can use a potential disaster to actually enhance the respectability of her mate. Because she is strong, solid and honorable and she speaks wisely, their relationship is strengthened and their ministry together improved.

Proverbs declares:

Through wisdom a house is built,
And by understanding it is established.

Proverbs 24:3, NKJ

A first lady knows that in order for she and her husband to serve as a cohesive team, there must be an understanding in the house. She must hold him up as her head and accept her place as his rib that walks alongside of him. In this way, together they can build a strong ministry for the advancement of the Kingdom of God.

If you can lay hold of this simple truth, you can be a great first lady.

Journal for Chapter 23

SCRIPTURE:

The wife must respect her husband. Ephesians 5:33

WORDS OF INSPIRATION:

A wife must learn humility toward her husband in all facets of their relationship. When there arises any issue that is hurtful for her, it's always better to wait until the two of them are alone and can communicate in private. She must always remember that he is the head of the household and that God has commanded that she respect him as such.

REFLECTIONS:

_____

_____

_____

_____

_____

_____

_____

_____

_____

Chapter Twenty-Four

Learning Where Dangers to Him Lurk

The wise are cautious and avoid danger;
fools plunge ahead with great confidence.

Proverbs 14:16, NLT

There are many areas where obvious dangers to your husband's welfare exist, but there are others that are not so obvious. These you have to learn and help him avoid. Some of the most cunning traps set for your husband are not in bars or nightclubs or in on-line chat rooms, but right within the very walls of the church. One of the areas where many pastors have been harmed is through intimate exchanges with other women during the course of counseling. Far too many pastors have fallen in this way.

The Groupie Mentality

It is beyond the scope of this book to explain in detail

why so many women are physically attracted to pastors, men of high standards, men of the cloth, just as other women are to rock stars, star athletes and movie stars. What needs to be said here is that it happens, and it happens a lot. Our concern need not be the why of it, but how to guard against it.

In the course of legitimate ministry to needy women, pastors have often proven vulnerable to temptation. They may have gone into this ministry with pure intentions, but at some point, human desires assert themselves, and the result is often tragic. Because of this, my contention is that when a pastor is counseling a woman (any woman), it's important for him to have his helpmate by his side. If a woman who needs counseling cannot or does not want to meet with both the pastor and the first lady, then something is wrong with that picture.

The Traps that Are Set

Some women who come in for counseling take the opportunity to speak about irrelevant things. More importantly, they often want to complain about their husband and how very much they are not pleased with him. They may even want to discuss with the pastor their husband's failures in the bedroom. This is not healthy.

Women suffering from female problems need prayer. They may have personal matters that would be more appropriately addressed by the first lady anyway, because, as a woman, she can understand those problems better. Sometimes the pastor doesn't need such specific information. His knowledge of the general problem is usually enough insight for him to know what and how to pray. He is a man of wisdom, and God can give him the words to pray without him having to know all the details.

Some women who come for prayer have suffered abuse and molestation, and as a result, they're experiencing low self-esteem and many other related problems. Or could they be on an assignment from the devil to destroy your home? It's very possible, so you need to be on guard.

Underlying Situations

In counseling, we often find that there are underlying situations that need to be addressed, and these may be legitimate. But some women just want to meet with the pastor to tell him their story. They cry on his shoulder and hug him, and he tells them it's going to be all right. This can be dangerous to everyone concerned.

Some women arrive for these counseling sessions wearing inappropriate clothing or they make provocative gestures toward the pastor. These actions are clearly intentional and absolutely unacceptable. For the purpose of establishing an atmosphere conducive for problem resolution and free from compromising and questionable interactions, the first lady needs to be present during these types of counseling sessions.

How Women See Their Pastor

Many women see their pastor on Sunday morning and/or during a midweek service, teaching and preaching the Word of God, and they begin to fantasize about what it would be like to be with him. They're already thinking in their hearts, "If I were the first lady, I would do this and have that." By requesting private counseling with the pastor, they either secretly or openly hope to tempt or actually seduce him.

Often this type of activity becomes a habit. Many women who come for counseling may truly be crying out for help, but they need someone to take a stance against the enemy who is working through them and to minister to them through wisdom and compassion. God has advised us in His Word:

Put on the whole armor of God, that you may be able to stand against the wiles of the devil.

Ephesians 6:11, NKJ

Seeking Whom They May Devour

Some of these women are very much like the enemy they so craftily serve. Peter warned:

Be careful! Watch out for attacks from the Devil, your great enemy. He prowls around like a roaring lion, looking for some victim to devour. Take a firm stand against him, and be strong in your faith. 1 Peter 5:8-9, NLT

Why would I be so bold as to say that some women are like Satan, *"looking for some victim to devour"*? It's because they actually move from church to church, repeating this process over and over again until they find a vulnerable victim or victims.

So what do they want? What are they looking for? It seems obvious to me that women like these will never be content until they have your husband. Once they realize that they can't get his attention, they usually move on quickly to seek another.

Their Tactics

Some try to use the first lady to get to her husband. They bring her gifts and want to take her out to eat or to do some shopping. And all the while, they're learning more about her husband and moving closer to him. They watch how the first lady acts and dresses, and then they try to emulate her. They are little more than wolves in sheep's clothing.

Suddenly, they want to help take care of the pastor's children, and so they offer to baby-sit or serve as a nanny for the family. This is just another way of getting into the pastor's home. Counseling such women alone, without the presence of the first lady, can easily spiral out of control and ultimately become disastrous.

Some of these women have endured a lot, and as a first lady, we must have compassion and love for them because we know what they truly desire is a real man to stand up to them. In their hearts, they hope the pastor will reject their temptations and minister to their spiritual needs. They are so accustomed to men misusing them and taking them for granted that they desperately need someone to stand up to them. Many pastors can't see this, and instead of taking a right stand, they fall into the trap she so cleverly sets.

My Research Bears Me Out

When researching this book, I discovered pastors who had counseled alone with women, only to find themselves in a very serious predicament. They started off caring about the person they were counseling (just as any pastor should), then, inadvertently, they fell in love with that other person. In some cases, they ended up divorcing their spouse and marrying the lady they counseled. This is a serious problem that needs to be addressed.

Every congregation must realize that their pastor and their first lady are one and that they work together as a team. Some women in the congregation are ministers themselves, and therefore they want to establish their own place in the ministry of the church. This desire definitely necessitates consulting with the pastor, but there's no reason that the pastor and first lady cannot assist such women ministers together. If everyone understands that this is the way things operate within the church, they will respect this order. After all, the pastor and first lady counseling together has many benefits, while his counseling alone can lead to unwarranted disaster. So let's not be afraid to use wisdom.

Finally, counseling is a very serious business, and pastors are spiritual counselors, not professional counselors. When it is needed, pastors and first ladies should feel free to refer their members to a professional, licensed counselor.

If you can lay hold of this simple truth, you can be a great first lady.

≈ Journal for Chapter 24 ≈

SCRIPTURE:

The wise are cautious and avoid danger;
fools plunge ahead with great confidence.

Proverbs 14:16, NLT

WORDS OF INSPIRATION:

Make the decision to always be present when your husband counsels other women. Counseling together is a wonderfully rewarding ministry, and allowing him to counsel other women alone may end in disaster.

REFLECTIONS:

_____

_____

_____

_____

_____

_____

_____

_____

_____

Chapter Twenty-Five

Learning to Minister to His Needs

A man leaves his father and mother and is joined to his wife, and the two are united into one.

Ephesians 5:31, NLT

Therefore, as God's chosen people, holy and dearly loved, clothe yourselves with compassion, kindness, humility, gentleness and patience. Bear with each other and forgive whatever grievances you may have against one another. Forgive as the Lord forgave you.

Colossians 3:12-13

After knowing God for yourself, marriage and the process of ministering to your husband can be a most wonderful and fulfilling experience. In marriage, we are called to minister to each other, but whether he upholds his end of the bargain or not, you should want to minister to his legitimate needs. If you fail in this, you might risk losing him, but your primary motivation, as a child of God, should be to please the Father.

Even though your husband is a minister and ministers to the needs of others, he himself has needs. And, since the two of you are one, when you minister to these needs, you are also ministering to yourself.

Examine Yourself First

Ministering to our husbands starts outside of the bedroom. It starts with an examination of your love for him.

In order to successfully and effectively minister to our husbands as the Word of God teaches, we must first examine our own motivations in marriage. What kind of love do you have for your husband? Is it materialistic: you love him as long as he spends money on you? Did you marry him for security? Do you love him in public, but not in private? Can you say that you love your husband unconditionally? That's the way God loves, and this is the kind of love He promotes and requires.

When we have unconditional love, it makes loving our husbands easy. Our love for him keeps on growing— even in the most difficult of times. Who wouldn't want to have that kind of love?

"But how can I have such love?" some might ask. Actually, it's a choice. We must *"clothe [ourselves] with compassion."* It's something that we choose to put on.

Be His Best Friend

Love that begins with friendship is healthy. Therefore a pastor's wife must be his very best friend. Best friends share things and demonstrate understanding of the other person's likes and dislikes. They listen to one another's hopes, disappointments, joys, fears, prayer requests, plans, ideas and interests. Friendship takes time to grow and develop, but it makes a love relationship much deeper and more satisfying. As you love and listen, you will minister to your husband's spirit.

Don't be so quick to share information with others about what may be going on in your household. When everything is back to normal, the family or friends whom you told will always remember what happened—even when peace and unity has returned to your home and you've forgotten it all yourself. Instead of telling others, take your troubles to God in prayer. Such confidentiality gives your husband security and ministers to his mind and spirit.

More than Friends

Since you are more than friends, it's always very important to display physical affection for your mate, not only in the bedroom, but at other times as well. Touching, holding hands, patting each other, hugging and kissing are all important ways to express your love for each other.

But there are other ways to turn him on. Try not to be so nagging and critical. Praise him in public, and then praise him even more in private. Learn to praise his strengths and to give his weaknesses to God. Compliment him. Pay attention to the way he gets his hair cut or the way his suit fits him. Ask him how his day went. Just paying attention to the small things about him goes a long way toward showing him how much he is loved.

Show him consideration by giving him his quiet time to meditate and regroup. Even that small respect is important and ministers to his soul.

Try This Little Exercise

Take a moment to do this little exercise. Because we know that *"death and life are in the power of the tongue"* (Proverbs 18:21, NKJ), practice speaking life into the character of your husband and into the romance of your marriage. Speak the following biblical passage aloud, replacing the words *he, his* or *him* with your husband's given name:

His eyes are like doves beside brooks of water; they are set like jewels.
His cheeks are like sweetly scented beds of spices.
His lips are like perfumed lilies.
His breath is like myrrh.
His arms are like round bars of gold, set with chrysolite.

His body is like bright ivory, aglow with sapphires.
His legs are like pillars of marble set in sockets of the
finest gold, strong as the cedars of Lebanon.
None can rival *him*.
His mouth is altogether sweet; *he* is lovely in every
way.
Such, O women of Jerusalem, is my lover, my friend.

Song of Solomon 5:12-16, NLT

Did it work for you? Do it enough, and it will begin
coming from your heart.

Your Assignment

Think of your husband as a God-given assignment
and know that it is your sole responsibility to help birth
the man God has ordained him to be. Study him and
learn new things about him. Find new and creative ways
to do something special for him. Being creative ministers
to him. No one else knows your king like you do.

The creative ways in which you can minister to your
husband are unlimited, and applying these few simple
principles and practices will increase your capacity to
minister to your husband's mind, body and soul.

If you can lay hold of this simple truth, you can be a
great first lady.

Journal for Chapter 25

SCRIPTURE:

Clothe yourselves with compassion, kindness, humility, gentleness and patience. Bear with each other and forgive whatever grievances you may have against one another. Forgive as the Lord forgave you.

Colossians 3:12-13

WORDS OF INSPIRATION:

God's Word tells us that we must never give up on people, especially the ones we say we love. It also tells us how to handle difficult situations, by activating the fruits of the Spirit in our own lives. This principle will bring peace and forgiveness to any marriage.

REFLECTIONS:

_____

_____

_____

_____

_____

_____

_____

Chapter Twenty-Six

Learning to Keep the Lines of Communication Open

Ears that hear and eyes that see—the Lord *has made them both.*   Proverbs 20:12

As we have noted, we first ladies are bombarded with so many daily pressures, including church, work and child-raising responsibilities, that it sometimes seems difficult for us to find the quality time needed for effective communication between husband and wife. Marital communication takes time, effort and planning, and when so many other things are pressing on us, it tends to be neglected. But we can't afford to let this happen because a healthy marriage depends upon open and honest communication.

Created for Communication

We were created to be harmonious and intimate communicators, first with God. But then He expects this gift also to be reflected in our interactions with one another. Generally, however, men are not the best communicators. Some men may even complain, "My wife acts like I'm being dragged, kicking and screaming, into every conversation." Why is it that marital communication sometimes seems to be a struggle?

We all encounter conditions that can hinder in-depth communication between spouses, and we all carry some baggage with us into our marriages. Could it be that our historical interactions with our parents or previous romantic interests have affected our ability to communicate in an uninhibited fashion? Other things frequently occupy our interests, like TV, the Internet and video games, isolating us from our spouse, family and friends. We get comfortable with these outside distractions, and then we allow them to rob us of important and necessary time investments in our most precious gift—the family.

Our Words Are Powerful

According to Proverbs 18:21, *"The tongue has the power of life and death, and those who love it will eat its fruit."* Could this be a reason we're not consistent with what we say and do for our husbands and ourselves? We can curse him with the same mouth with which we praise God.

Our words are extremely powerful to the man with whom we fell in love. Why not use them to edify and build him up, thereby assisting him in his ministry and his walk with God? Our men need us to understand, support and be there for them. Never risk using words that can inflict pain on him. Remember, this is the man God gave you to nurture and stand beside.

Speak Healing Words

God gives us the power to speak healing words into our marriages, rather than words that cause pain. Verbally express your appreciation. Compliment him. Praise him. Speak the language of love.

Then allow him to talk, while you simply listen. Give him your undivided attention. Affirm his thoughts with responses such as, "I understand" and "I see your point" or "That sounds like something we can work on." Never send him away feeling that he was not heard or understood. Communication is both talking and listening, and both are vital to your marriage and your life. An ability to listen will greatly benefit any marriage for years to come.

Help your marriage to grow with open communication and understanding. Husbands are commanded to do it:

Husbands, likewise, dwell with them with understanding.   1 Peter 3:7, NKJ

If this is important for husbands, it's equally important for us. So, don't give up! Allow God to work the communication issue out in your marriage, and know that He has a plan for both you and your husband. To emphasize, His plan includes the both of you. In order for God's plan to come to fruition, you and your husband must be one, walking in total agreement. Communicating is the key to retaining the vitality and one-accordness in your marriage.

If you can lay hold of this simple truth, you can be a great first lady.

Journal for Chapter 26

SCRIPTURE:

Ears that hear and eyes that see—the LORD has made them both.   Proverbs 20:12

WORDS OF INSPIRATION:

Listen to your spouse. Be attentive. Repeat in your own words what you heard him say so that he knows you're listening and desire to understand what he's saying. Then, be prepared to act on what you've heard.

REFLECTIONS:

_____
_____
_____
_____
_____
_____
_____
_____
_____
_____
_____

Chapter Twenty-Seven

Learning the Secret Places of a First Lady

The secret things belong to the LORD our God.
Deuteronomy 29:29, NKJ

"The secret things." What are they? In ministry, there are many, and unless they are kept secret, you can do serious damage to yourself, your husband, your church and the Kingdom of God as a whole. *"The secret things"* are things that no one else can know about. And why is that? It's because God has called you to this exalted position, and if these things were to become known, others might not respect you as they should and must.

What Are Your Secrets?

Pastors are human, and as such, they are susceptible to fail and to exhibit human frailties. It is not uncommon to learn from pastor's wives, for example, that they have been mentally, physically or verbally abused by their husband at some point. Some pastors have been known to drink, to smoke, to use profanity or to indulge in pornography.

Some pastors go further and actually become womanizers. Some first ladies discover, to their great sadness, that they're not really the only lady in their husband's life. In some cases, they're little more than a cover for him. They're still there only because of being his legal wife and the mother of his children. That's a hard burden for any woman to bear.

Some pastors have been known to begin living a down-low life-style. So what can his wife do? She should pray for him. Any time a pastor is not really living the life that he calls others to, it's a problem. He may begin to deal falsely with others. It may be that the church has become just another business for him, not a place to win souls and change lives.

Problems with Wives and Children

First ladies are not always the innocent victims. Sometimes the men of the church shower her with way too much attention, and their motives are not good. If she is emotionally moved by their advances, bad things can happen. More often than not, it's the pastor who strays.

Are pastors neglecting the physical needs of their family? Does their wife go to service each week wearing the same drab garments? Are the children suffering?

Sometimes it's the children themselves who are the problem. For instance, in some cases, a pastor's children have been seen out clubbing and doing drugs with friends. These are clearly family problems that must be dealt with, but the average believer doesn't have the where-withal to deal with them or to help in any way. Rather than help, they would be scandalized and perhaps leave the faith themselves. At the very least, they would speak to others of these things, thus doing grave damage to the pastor, the church and its outreaches.

These are the kinds of things I'm referring to as *"the secret things."* Unless there is someone over you who can deal with them effectively, give them to God and know that He can resolve them better than any living person.

The Larger Family

Not all of the things we must guard as secrets involve our personal family. They may involve the larger church family. When dealing with large numbers of people, we always have those who are disrespectful or disobedient or worse. Should we publish this news so that everyone will revile that person and send them fleeing from the church back into the world? Or should we pray for them, show them love and believe for them to be restored and affirmed? The Scriptures are strong on this point:

Brethren, if a man is overtaken in any trespass, you who are spiritual restore such a one in a spirit of gentleness, considering yourself lest you also be tempted.

Galatians 6:1, NKJ

It would be easy for a first lady to dismiss a person who has shown her disrespect in some way, but then again, these are our children, just as much as those to whom we gave physical birth. A first lady cannot afford to hold any grudges. She, more than anyone in the church, must forgive and work toward restoration for that person.

Your "Secret Things"

"The secret things." You may not have experienced these same issues, but all of us have something we're not free to divulge. What is your secret? It might be something so terribly convoluted that no one else could possibly understand it. What's important to remember is that *"the secret things belong to the LORD."* Give them to Him, and trust Him to deal with them.

In this way, you become a covering for your husband, for your family and for the body of believers entrusted to your care. Your personal prayer time need not be consumed with the things that trouble you. This might lead to you being depressed and feeling down and out, worried, sad, lonely and confused. Your head should be up at all times, never down. You should be free to concentrate on ministry, not be burdened down with misery. You're a woman, like any other, and you have your own needs, desires, dreams and goals—just as all women do. You, too, need encouragement and prayer, and you can only hope that someone will pick up the banner of prayer for you.

But, whether others help you carry the burden or not, always remember that God knows about all of your secrets, and He will see you through. He will never place upon you any more than you can bear. Psalm 55 reminds us:

> *Cast your cares on the* Lord *and he will sustain you;*
> *he will never let the righteous fall.*   Psalm 55:22

Your burden may be great at times, but you can handle it. You may need to do some fasting and praying, but know that the Lord will hear you and answer.

Join a Support Group

I recommend that all first ladies join a support group consisting of other first ladies, and if none exists near you, why not establish one? This will give you someone you can talk to, someone who may be experiencing struggles similar to your own. Through support groups like this, we can pray together, share together and be reminded that we are not alone. Through our Lord Jesus Christ, we have the victory.

If you can lay hold of this simple truth, you can be a great first lady.

Journal for Chapter 27

SCRIPTURE:

The secret things belong to the LORD our God.

Deuteronomy 29:29, NKJ

WORDS OF INSPIRATION:

We can go to God about our *"secret things,"* and there we can pour out all our most intimate needs to Him. We know that He will hear us, He will comfort us and assure us that everything will be all right. And He will change the situations we need changed.

REFLECTIONS:

_____

_____

_____

_____

_____

_____

_____

_____

_____

My Prayer For You Today,
Dear First Lady

Dear God,

I thank You for my sister in Christ, and I ask for Your favor to continue to be with her. I ask for Your protection to cover her. I thank You, Lord, for Your grace, love, power and mercy upon her today.

Lord, give her peace and joy. Direct her path. Give her wisdom and understanding. Give her the strength she so desperately needs.

Lord, grant her good character, patience and long-suffering. Help her, Lord, to be the godly lady whom You have called her to be. Help her to be the pastor's wife You have chosen for this day and hour.

Bless her family and equip her for her task. Lord, I pray blessings over my sister's life today.

In the name of Jesus,
Amen!

Appendices

Appendix 1

A First Lady's Poem

by Lady Gayle Woodard

First is to be in front, not behind.
We must stay ahead, no lagging behind.
A lady that leads, she's always ready
Because she knows she has to start first.
She's serving so that others can follow.
As they see her serve, so will they also.
A lady of class, that lady that God chose to pilot her congregation,
Because He knows she will guide with power and love,
compassion, long suffering, gentleness and kindness.
Who's that lady?
God said, "She's the Lady I chose."

Appendix 2

Which Would Describe You?

As a pastor's wife, which of the following characters would best describe you?

ABIGAIL:

You might be in the position of Abigail. She had a fool for a husband, but she had the wisdom to cover him. Nabel was a rich man, yet unsaved and very insensitive. However, Abigail had wisdom, and she was not in denial about her husband. She stood up for what was right. Her character showed godliness. She spoke words of poetry. She was sensitive and beautiful. I would describe her as a woman of wisdom, beauty and class.

JOB'S WIFE:

Job was a man who feared the Lord. He was blameless and shunned evil and had great integrity. Through all the suffering and pain he had to endure, he never sinned against God. His wife however, was a foolish woman. She wanted him to curse God and die. Does that sound like you? God will always reward us in our sufferings, so don't ever give up on Him.

QUEEN ESTHER:

God will prepare you for your purpose, just as He favored Esther. She was an orphan girl, but she had much faith and demonstrated leadership abilities. She gave instructions to her people to fast and pray for three days before she went before the king. She was a woman of faith and royal bearing and had great confidence in what she believed.

Esther was a Jewish woman, and stood strong for her people. When she approached the king, it could have cost her her life—if he had refused her. But when we walk in humility and integrity before God, He will take care of us.

Appendix 3

My Song For You, First Lady

Nobody knows but You, Lord.
Nobody knows but You, Lord.
Nobody knows but You.

The many prayers that I prayed,
The many tears that I shed,

Lord, I need Your power.
Lord, I need Your love.
Lord, I need Your strength.

Thank You, Lord.
Thank You, Lord.

You are so good to me. You're my Jehovah Jireh, my
God Almighty.

Thank You, Lord, for Your love and power.
Nobody knows but You, Lord.

Appendix 4

More about the Author

Gayle Woodard is the First Lady of the CRM City Fellowship church in Houston, Texas, where she walks alongside her husband, Pastor Leroy Woodard, Jr., of twenty-three years in ministry. CRM is one church with three locations.

Gayle is a native Houstonian and a graduate of Robert E. Lee High School. She attended the University of Houston, where she majored in Business and later attended Houston Community College, where she received her Cosmetology License. She has recently opened a cutting-edge salon located at the CRM church in the Woodlands.

First Lady Gayle Woodard is the proud mother of two sons: Leroy Woodard II is currently a Business Administration major, a sophomore in college and Demond Woodard is currently a junior in high school.

Gayle is also the Director of the CRM Women's Ministry, where her passion is reaching out to hurting women of all ages, sizes and colors. She also mentors girls. She has such a heart for women that she reached out into the community and founded the Koinonia Sorority, "Women Helping Women Overcome." This organization helps restore and transform women's lives domestically, professionally and educationally, while uplifting their self-esteem. It mentors girls to become powerful young ladies through seminars and other educational programs. It empowers, rebuilds and makes a difference in the lives of women and girls.

Lady Gayle also joins her husband, Pastor Leroy Woodard, Jr., one of the chosen hosts for Daystar Television, with founders Marcus and Joni Lamb, to spread the Word of God, encouraging many through the television ministry. She stands alongside of her husband, not only in church ministry, but also serves in the community with the distribution of clothing, food, toys, utilities and much more. Together they operate the citywide Club of Clubs, a nonprofit organization which feeds thousands of people at the George R. Brown Convention Center in Houston, Texas, during Thanksgiving and Christmas. Those who come there receive hot meals with all the trimmings. They also get the privilege to take home food baskets and toys for their children. They are able to receive their flu shots, free haircuts and free long-distance calls during the holiday season ... and much, much more. This woman loves to serve others.

Lady Gayle Woodard also founded Gayle's Gems and Group, a group that goes out into the community to serve the needs of senior citizens. She wants these seniors to know that they're not forgotten, so every year, during the holidays, she and the team take baskets to their homes. Gayle's Gems and Group travel to the north, south, east and west of the city of Houston, to share with needy seniors wherever they find them. The faces of these people light up when they receive their baskets. Then the team prays with them and takes photos together. If the people have some serious need, it is noted so that someone from the ministry can see that it is filled.

Gayle's Gem and Group also takes toys to children in the hospital during the holiday season, to lift their spirits. She considers it to be a blessing to serve others in women's shelters, girl's homes and wherever she sees a need. The list goes on and on. This anointed woman of God is making a difference in the lives of many.

Last, but not least, Lady Gayle Woodard is a songwriter.

Ministry Page

Readers may contact the author through any of the following addresses:

CRM City Fellowship Church
One Church, Three Locations
(713) 659-7750

Konionia Sorority
kwssorority@yahoo.com
(713) 655-7550

First Ladies Support Group
Supporting the Call
"A Friend Indeed"
Taking Off the Mask of Ministry

Perfume and incense bring joy to the heart and the pleasantness of one's friends springs from his earnest counsel!   Proverbs 29:7

To join, email us at firstladiesgroup@yahoo.com.

Notes

Notes

CPSIA information can be obtained at www.ICGtesting.com
Printed in the USA
LVOW08s1336311013

359465LV00001B/15/P